CHILDREN'S ENGLISH AND SERVICES STUDY

EDUCATIONAL NEEDS ASSESSMENT FOR LANGUAGE MINORITY CHILDREN WITH LIMITED ENGLISH PROFICIENCY

J. Michael O'Malley

ACKNOWLEDGMENTS

This study represents a striking example of successful collaboration among Federal agencies and of cooperation between Federal and State agencies concerned with education research and language minority issues. The study was largely funded by the National Institute of Education with a contribution from the National Center for Education Statistics, and with additional contributions from the U.S. Office of Bilingual Education and the Assistant Secretary for Planning and Evaluation in the Department of Health, Education, and Welfare. State Education Agencies contributed staff time to advise the Federal agencies on the design of essential components of the study. The study was monitored by NIE with technical assistance from NCES. Comments and suggestions on the draft reports were provided by the Interagency Part C Committee on Bilingual Research, and the results of the household survey were reviewed under contract with NCES.

For their contributions to the development and design of the study, the following individuals must be acknowledged. Leslie Silverman of NCES was a continual source of energy and of confidence that the imposing technical obstacles could be overcome, while often indicating the path which led to their solution. His colleague at NCES, Dorothy Waggoner, was a strong contributor to the design stage of the study through her familiarity with language surveys and bilingual education. The Chief State School Officers of many (roughly 30) States freed time for their senior staff to serve on a review team for the study. Some of those staff who contributed most heavily, particularly to the design of the language instrument, were José Martínez of California, Ernest Mazzone of Massachusetts, María Ramírez of New York, Elena Vergara of Indiana, and Robin Johnston of Colorado.

This list of acknowledgments would not be complete without a sincere expression of gratitude to the participating language minority children and their families and to the schools in which the children were enrolled.

This document is published by InterAmerica Research Associates, Inc., pursuant to contract NIE 400–80–0040 to operate the National Clearinghouse for Bilingual Education. The National Clearinghouse for Bilingual Education is jointly funded by the National Institute of Education and the Office of Bilingual Education and Minority Languages Affairs, U.S. Department of Education. Contractors undertaking such projects under government sponsorship are encouraged to express their judgment freely in professional and technical matters; the views expressed in this publication do not necessarily reflect the views of the sponsoring agencies.

InterAmerica Research Associates, Inc. d/b/a
National Clearinghouse for Bilingual Education
1300 Wilson Boulevard, Suite B2-11
Rosslyn, Virginia 22209
(703) 522-0710 / (800) 336-4560

ISBN: 0–89763–088–2
First Printing 1982
Printed in USA

10 9 8 7 6 5 4 3 2 1

CONTENTS

LIST OF TABLES

FOREWORD

This report is the second of two documents presenting the results of the Children's English and Services Study (CESS), a national investigation of educational needs and services conducted with language minority students with limited English proficiency. The first document, *Language Minority Students with Limited English Proficiency* (O'Malley, 1981), reported estimated numbers of limited English proficient students aged 5–14 years by age, language background, and area of the country. The present volume contains information on the educational needs of these students and on the school services provided to them. An executive summary of the first report appears in the Appendix.

The study, sponsored by the National Institute of Education and the National Center for Education Statistics, represents the first time that a number of important methodological refinements over previous investigations converged. No previous national survey had specifically designed a sample to improve the yield of language minority households. This was done not only in the interest of efficiency, to avoid screening excessively large numbers of households, but also because a general sample could too easily have missed important segments of the United States where language minorities are located. Before this study, no investigation had attempted to develop a single definition of limited English proficiency that was acceptable to both bilingual practitioners and State Education Agencies and conformed to the definition in Federal legislation. The study also represents the first occasion for obtaining national information on school services provided to limited English proficient, language minority children and the first time when indicators of educational need have been identified on a national sample of language minority students.

J. Michael O'Malley is project director for the 1980–1981 Teachers Languages Skills Survey, a study designed to determine the number of teachers in the United States who have the appropriate language skills and background to offer instruction to limited English proficient children. The project is administered by InterAmerica Research Associates through support from the Office of Bilingual Education and Minority Languages Affairs in the U.S. Department of Education. Dr. O'Malley has been research consultant and director for various projects and evaluative studies in the areas of early childhood education, bilingual education, and youth employment. While a senior research associate at the National Institute of Education, he was project officer for the Children's English and Services Study.

One of the activities of the National Clearinghouse for Bilingual Education is to publish documents addressing the specific information needs of the bilingual education community. We are pleased to make this title available through our growing list of publications. Subsequent Clearinghouse products will similarly seek to contribute information that can assist in the education of minority language and culture groups in the United States.

National Clearinghouse
for Bilingual Education

EXECUTIVE SUMMARY

EDUCATIONAL NEEDS ASSESSMENT FOR LANGUAGE MINORITY CHILDREN WITH LIMITED ENGLISH PROFICIENCY

SPRING 1978

In Spring 1978, fewer than six percent of children aged 5–14 who were from non-English language backgrounds and who were limited in English proficiency (LEP) received bilingual instruction that constituted minimum acceptable services. These findings were based on a national household survey of language minorities in the United States, including school data on children living in those households.[1]

The study design followed the specifications of an external review group composed of representatives of State Education Agencies (SEAs). Chief State School Officers in all 50 States had been asked to designate a person to serve on the review group who could represent the SEA views on bilingual education and language minority children. Among those designated to serve on the review team were State Directors of Bilingual Education or their designates, members of the Committee on Evaluation and Information Systems of the Council of Chief State School Officers, and other persons involved in bilingual education, language assessment, or data collection systems in the State. In all, 30 States were represented throughout the series of advisory group meetings that spanned the life of the project. The group was responsible primarily for establishing criteria to define limited English proficiency among language minorities and for developing specifications to collect information on school services provided to language minority students.

Limited English proficiency was established in the survey through a specially constructed test of speaking, understanding, reading, and writing in English, individually administered to children. Criteria used to define minimum acceptable services in this study were formulated by the task force. According to the task force, minimum acceptable services for language minority children consisted of:

1. Assessment of proficiency in English and the non-English languages

2. A minimum of five hours per week instruction each in English and non-English languages

3. Professional staffing in all instruction.

Additional findings covered the types of instructional services the schools provided, the proportion of limited English proficient, language minority children who received bilingual or other special language services, the number of task force criteria that were met or not met by available services, and the unmet educational needs of limited English proficient children. General findings were:

1. Services provided to LEP children varied, depending on the specific criteria designated by the task force.

---

1. The report is based on information from California, New York, and the remainder of the country. Data were not available for Texas. Sample sizes and response rates restrict the interpretation of the findings, as discussed later in this report.

2. Nearly all LEP children were taught by an individual considered to be a professional by the certification and hiring policies of the school district.

3. Schools appeared to be concentrating available resources on the students who were most in need.

4. LEP children were described as more often below grade level in reading achievement, more frequently retained in grade, and more frequently overaged in grade than language minority children whose English proficiency was not limited.

GENERAL CHARACTERISTICS OF INSTRUCTION FOR LIMITED ENGLISH PROFICIENT STUDENTS

Educational services provided to language minority children in the study were classified as bilingual when language arts or content-area instruction was offered in or through the child's native language. The services were classified as English as a second language (ESL) when special forms of English instruction were provided. Services were classified as standard, English-medium instruction when the child was taught with no apparent effort to accommodate the student's English language proficiency or background. Findings apply to language minority children aged 5–14 in all areas of the country except Texas. Major findings were the following:

- An estimated 23% of all language minority children with limited English proficiency received instruction bilingually either in content areas or in language arts instruction of a non-English language.

- Approximately 11% of all language minority children with limited English proficiency received English as a second language (ESL) instruction, apart from those children who may have received ESL instruction along with bilingual instruction.

- An estimated 58% of limited English proficient children from language minority backgrounds received standard, English-medium instruction, and 7% received some other form of instruction not described by the above categories.

- Of the limited English proficient children who received bilingual instruction, 54% were in grades K–3, 29% were in grades 4–6, and 17% were in grades 7–9. In comparison, of the language minority children who were *not* limited in English proficiency (as defined by this study's criteria) and who received English-medium instruction, 36% were in grades K–3, 37% were in grades 4–6, and 26% were in grades 7–9.

- An estimated 24% of all limited English proficient, language minority children received instruction under Federal support from ESEA Title I (Compensatory Education); 7%, from ESEA Title VII (Bilingual Education); and less than 5%, from any single other Federal source.

- State bilingual support for instruction was received by an estimated 14% of the limited English proficient, language minority students, while 12% received other State support.

TARGETED SERVICES FOR LIMITED ENGLISH PROFICIENT, LANGUAGE MINORITY CHILDREN

The results of the CESS school survey identified the proportion of LEP, language minority children aged 5–14 receiving language-related instructional services compared with those who were not limited in English language proficiency, but who were also receiving services. The results were as follows:

- An estimated 82% of language minority children receiving bilingual types of instruction were limited in English proficiency.

- An estimated 83% of all language minority children receiving English as a second language instruction were limited in English proficiency.

- An estimated 79% of all language minority children receiving instruction under Federal ESEA Title I (Compensatory Education) support were limited in English language proficiency.

- An estimated 83% of all language minority children receiving Federal support from ESEA Title VII (Bilingual Education) were limited in English proficiency.

- An estimated 75% of all language minority children receiving State bilingual support for instruction were limited in English proficiency, and 76% of those receiving local bilingual support for instruction were limited in English proficiency.

TASK FORCE CRITERIA FOR ADEQUACY OF INSTRUCTIONAL SERVICES

Services provided to limited English proficient children varied, depending on the specific criteria designated by the task force of State Education Agency officials. The criteria were formulated in terms of three characteristics of instruction: staff qualifications, clock hours of instruction per week in English and non-English languages, and type of assessment administered in English and non-English languages. In all results which follow, English as a second language and standard, English-medium instruction are grouped as English-medium instruction.

- An estimated 96% of all limited English proficient children received instruction from a person designated by the school as a qualified teaching professional. This figure was slightly higher for bilingual and English-medium instruction, but dropped to 57% for limited English proficient children receiving other forms of instruction.

- Five or more hours per week of instruction in English were received by an estimated 83% of the limited English proficient children in bilingual instruction, 76% of those students enrolled in English-medium instruction, and 35% in other forms of instruction.

- Five or more hours' instruction in non-English languages were received by an estimated 71% of the limited English proficient students in bilingual instruction, 8% of those in English-medium instruction, and 4% of those in other forms of instruction.

- Of the total population of limited English proficient children, approximately 17% received bilingual instruction that was acceptable for the task force specifications on hours of non-English language use.

- In bilingual instruction programs, tests to assess English language proficiency were administered to an estimated 44% of the language minority children, and tests to assess non-English language proficiency were administered to an estimated 23% of the language minority children.

- In English-medium settings, tests to assess English language proficiency were administered to an estimated 29% of the language minority students, and tests to assess non-English language proficiency were administered to an estimated 12% of the language minority students.

- Of the total population of language minority children, approximately 10% received English language assessment acceptable by task force specifications for a bilingual setting, and about 6% received non-English language assessment in a bilingual instructional setting that met the task force specifications.

EDUCATIONAL NEEDS OF LANGUAGE MINORITY CHILDREN

The study used four indices to reflect the overall extent to which school services provided to language minority children were responsive to student educational needs:

1. Subject area assessment administered in reading, math, and other areas

2. School classification of needs of students designated to be limited in English proficiency according to an external test criterion

3. School-reported level of reading achievement

4. School-designated grade retention and overagedness in grade.

The results are reported in the aggregate for all instructional types:

- An estimated 62% of the limited English proficient children received assessment of reading in English. Approximately 57% received English-language assessment in math. The percentages for non-limited English proficient children did not differ appreciably. There were no marked differences from these estimates for children with Spanish compared with all other language backgrounds combined.

- An estimated 5% of the limited English proficient children received assessment of reading in non-English languages. These results were similar to those for assessments administered in math and other areas in non-English languages, and differed little for children from Spanish compared with all other language backgrounds combined.

- An estimated 22% of the limited English proficient children were rated by schools as able to use English very well, 19% as able to use English adequately, and 14% as slightly limited; 34% were not rated at all. These results showed little difference by language background of the child.

- Schools rated an estimated 52% of the limited English proficient children as being one-half year or more below grade level in reading in English. In comparison, only 12% of non-limited English proficient, language minority children were rated below grade level in reading to the same degree.

- Schools reported that an estimated 11% of all limited English proficient students repeated at least one grade or course, in comparison with about 2% for non-limited English proficient, language minority children. Figures for different language groups were roughly comparable.

- Schools reported an estimated 9% of the total limited English proficient population to be 2 or more years older than the age expected for children in their grade level.

SOURCE OF DATA

The Children's English and Services Study was conducted under contract from the National Institute of Education with shared support from the National Center for Education Statistics and other agencies in the U.S. Department of Education. The study was designed to respond to Congressional mandates in the Bilingual Education Act (Elementary and Secondary Education Act, Title VII) to estimate the number of children with limited English speaking ability in the United States, and to determine the educational needs of limited English proficient children. The work was carried out by a consortium headed by L. Miranda and Associates, Inc., of Washington, D.C. as prime contractor.

Adults were interviewed in the Spring of 1978 in a nationally representative sample of approximately 35,000 households. About 2,200 households were identified where a language other than English was spoken and where children between the ages of 5 and 14 were living. Within these households, selected children were individually administered a test in English that determined whether or not they were limited in English language proficiency. A questionnaire was sent to the schools to identify educational needs of children enrolled. The sample was designed to provide representative numbers of children in California, Texas, New York, and in the remainder of the country; however, school information for Texas is not reported because of a low response rate.

The test in English was designed to meet the definition of limited English proficiency in the Bilingual Education Act. Representatives of 30 State Education Agencies served on a review team for the study and developed specifications for the test. The reviewers found that no existing test would meet the Congressional intent, and urged development of a test measuring age-specific speaking, listening, reading, and writing skills in English. The identification of limited English proficiency is a cut-off point of the total score that accurately classifies children as limited or not limited in English for their age level. The criterion for this score was school district determination of limited English proficiency, derived from field work with an independent sample. The State reviewers also specified the school questionnaire designed to determine educational needs and school services, based on criteria for acceptable provision of services which they developed and agreed upon.

The Children's English and Services Study is one of a number of studies being undertaken by the U.S. Department of Education to assess educational needs of and to improve instructional effectiveness for limited English proficient children.

ACCURACY OF THE DATA

The results of this study are based on a sample. All figures provided in this report are estimates of what would be obtained with a complete census. Response rates and accuracy of data for the household survey are discussed in a report prepared by the contractor (Miranda, 1979b). The response rate on the school survey for California, New York, and the remainder of the country except for Texas was 67%. The school survey results should be taken only as suggestive because of the level of nonresponse and the variation in school practice that could result from responses to a mail-out questionnaire. Additionally, it should be kept in mind that the level of services reported are for LEP and NLEP students as determined by a test specially constructed for this study. The identification of LEP and NLEP students based on this test does not necessarily agree with the various procedures used in each school site. Consequently, the level and type of services provided to students in the study may reflect differences in identification procedures used in various communities.

I. INTRODUCTION

Limited English proficient children have been the focus of Federal and State legislation in bilingual education and of a Supreme Court decision directing schools not to discriminate against national origin minority children on the basis of English language proficiency. Consequently, for the past several years the U.S. Department of Education has performed a series of studies to determine the educational needs of language minorities living in the United States. School-age children with limited proficiency in English are of particular concern in these studies.

Through these investigations, the Department of Education has attempted to answer questions about the level and type of educational services appropriate for limited English proficient children. The questions are of the following kind: First, how many children are there with limited proficiency in English? In the absence of information on the total number of children, projections to establish appropriate levels of services would be based on speculation. Second, what are the educational needs of limited English proficient children? Beyond the count of children, projections of future service requirements should take into account the special needs these children may have. Third, what types of services are required for children whose needs are not being addressed? Specific information about types of programs available and staffing requirements is needed.

A report on the number of limited English proficient children living in the United States has been published by the National Clearinghouse for Bilingual Education under the title *Children's English and Services Study: Language Minority Children with Limited English Proficiency in the United States* (O'Malley, 1981). According to the report, in the Spring of 1978 there were 2.4 million language minority background children aged 5–14 years with limited English language proficiency in the United States. This represents 63% of all children aged 5–14 living in households where a language other than English was spoken. The present report adds to the count the results of an educational needs assessment for limited English proficient children.

Legislative Mandates

The needs assessment for limited English proficient students was first mandated in the Bilingual Education Act as amended in 1974 (Title VII of the Elementary and Secondary Education Act). The needs assessment was required in the Bilingual Education Act as part of a report on the condition of bilingual education in the Nation to be submitted by the Commissioner of Education, which would include:

> A national assessment of the educational needs of children and other persons with limited English-speaking ability and of the extent to which such needs are being met by Federal, State, and local efforts, including (A) . . . the results of a survey of the number of such children and persons in the States. (Section 731 [C][1])

In the Education Amendments of 1974, Congress went on to mandate the count by the National Center for Education Statistics (NCES):

> The National Center for Education Statistics shall conduct the survey required by Section 731(C)(A) of Title VII of the Elementary and Secondary Education Act. (Section 501 [B][A])

At the same time, the Bilingual Education Act required the National Institute of Education (NIE) to "determine the basic educational needs of children with limited English speaking ability" in section 742 (C)(1).

In combination, the Congressional mandates to identify needs and services for the Commissioner's report, to count limited English speaking children, and to determine basic educational needs constituted an extensive effort to obtain information to support policy decisions in bilingual education. The count of limited English proficient children and the educational needs assessment were the basis for attempts to establish the scope of bilingual education in future revisions of the Bilingual Education Act.

Prior Research to Count Limited English Proficient Children

A series of coordinated studies within the Education Department has been completed to count limited English proficient children. The following discussion traces the direction of those efforts, and identifies their relationship to the mandated needs assessment.

Survey of Income and Education (SIE). The SIE was the major NCES response to the mandated survey. The SIE was required in the Education Amendments of 1974 to furnish current data on the number of school-age children in poverty for purposes of formula allocation of ESEA Title I support. By cooperative agreement with the Bureau of the Census, which conducted the SIE, NCES included language questions on the SIE household interview and supplemented the SIE sample in selected States wherever necessary to provide acceptably accurate State-level estimates of language minority persons of school age. In a series of reports, NCES indicated the geographic distribution, country of origin, and school enrollment status of language minorities based on the SIE (National Center for Education Statistics, 1978a, 1978b, 1978c, 1979). The SIE language questions concentrated on language background, usage, and English proficiency. Because detailed information on these language characteristics had not been collected previously on a national scale, extensive development work on the language questions was required to carry out the response to the mandate. The following describes this work.

Survey of Languages. The Survey of Languages had two purposes. It was a pilot survey for questions on language characteristics and place of birth for the SIE, and it provided preliminary estimates of language background characteristics at the national level. The Survey of Languages was a supplement to the July 1975 Current Population Survey (CPS), a household survey performed monthly by the Bureau of the Census for the U.S. Department of Labor to obtain employment estimates and other information about the labor force. In the Survey of Languages, alternative interpretations of the legislative definition of "language minority" were developed and tested. Each interpretation yielded an estimate of the number of language minorities, among whom would be found persons with limited English-speaking ability. These estimates were de-

scribed in the first *Commissioner's Report on the Condition of Bilingual Education in the Nation* in November 1976.

Measure of English Language Proficiency (MELP). In the SIE, direct assessment of the language proficiency of school-age children from language minority backgrounds was not possible. The Bureau of the Census wished to maintain a household interview format on the SIE and prohibited the use of paper-and-pencil tests, electronic recordings, or direct interviews of each household member in the sample. Thus, field work separate from the SIE was needed to identify a set of census-type questions that would predict English language proficiency as a surrogate for more thorough assessment. This set of census-type questions constituted the MELP. In the field work, performed under contract with the National Center for Education Statistics (Hartwell et al., 1976; Stolz and Bruck, 1976), the assessment criteria were an English language proficiency test, direct ratings by the interviewer of the child's English language proficiency, and school district classification of language minority children as either limited or proficient in English-speaking ability. The method for predicting English language proficiency from the MELP was based on correlational techniques and procedures that maximized accurate classifications when predicting the assessment criterion. Simulations of the prediction in the field test revealed that questions on language usage and skill in speaking and understanding English were useful in the prediction. However, it was also found that MELP items varied depending on the proportion of limited English speaking children in the language minority group. Because the proportion was then unknown, a separate study was required for the MELP in the SIE to be useful in providing State-level estimates of the number of limited English speaking children.

Children's English and Services Study (CESS)

By interagency agreement among the National Institute of Education (NIE), the National Center for Education Statistics (NCES) and other agencies in the U.S. Department of Education, a study to determine the proportion of language minority children with limited English proficiency was performed by L. Miranda and Associates, Inc. (LM&A) of Washington, D.C. as prime contractor. Westat of Rockville, Maryland and Resource Development Institute of Austin, Texas were LM&A's major subcontractors in the consortium (Miranda, 1979a, 1979b). The study was titled the *Children's English and Services Study* (CESS) (O'Malley, 1981).

In addition to providing estimates of the proportion of language minority children with limited English proficiency, the CESS was designed to provide estimates of the number of limited English speaking children from Spanish language backgrounds and the aggregate of all other language minorities combined in major geographic sections of the United States.

The CESS used a sample of households in which a language other than English was spoken usually or often, consistent with the CPS and SIE definitions. Responses to the MELP questions were collected from adult respondents for children aged 5–14 in those households. The external criterion for limited English proficiency among these children was an individually administered test of speaking, understanding, reading, and writing in English constructed especially for this study. Children whose scores on the instrument fell below a criterion score were designated as limited in English proficiency (LEP), while children whose scores fell at or above the criterion score were considered non-limited in English proficiency (NLEP).[2]

Determining the proportion of children with limited English proficiency and estimating

numbers of limited English proficient children were the primary purpose of the CESS. This information was based on the CESS household survey, completed in Spring 1978. Results and details on the methodology for the household survey are contained in O'Malley (1981). Results are reported for two language groups (Spanish, all others), four age groups (5–6, 7–8, 9–11, and 12–14), and four geographic areas (California, Texas, New York, and the remainder of the country).

CESS Needs Assessment

A secondary purpose of the CESS was to respond to the mandated needs assessment in bilingual education—that is, to determine "the extent to which . . . (educational) needs are being met by Federal, State, and Local efforts." The CESS also was designed to respond in part to the NIE mandate to "determine the basic educational needs of children with limited English speaking ability." To meet these mandates, a pupil survey was designed which followed specifications established by the CESS advisory groups. The survey questionnaire was mailed to schools enrolling language minority children aged 5–14 in the CESS household sample. The pupil survey was completed in Spring 1979. The present report presents the conceptual framework and survey methodology for estimating educational needs of limited English proficient children based on the pupil survey. The results indicate the types of educational needs that characterize limited English proficient children and the types of instructional services the students receive.

---

2. For a discussion of the cutoff score see *Children's English and Services Study: Estimates of Limited English Proficient Children in the United States— Methodological Reviews*, published by the National Clearinghouse for Bilingual Education (Rosslyn, Virginia), 1982.

II. CONCEPTUAL FRAMEWORK AND SURVEY METHODS FOR ESTIMATING EDUCATIONAL NEEDS OF AND SERVICES FOR LIMITED ENGLISH PROFICIENT CHILDREN

In the Children's English and Services Study (CESS), English language assessment of a sample of 1,909 language minority children in a **household survey** provided information on the number of limited English proficiency children aged 5–14 years. A **pupil survey completed by the schools** provided information about educational needs of and instructional services provided to a sample of approximately 1,000 language minority children.

This section of the report focuses on the pupil survey and describes the conceptual framework for the needs assessment, specifications for the survey questionnaire, the field data collection effort, and response rates. Detail on this information is provided elsewhere in Appendix A.

Conceptual Framework

The framework for the educational needs assessment was tied to the count of limited English proficient children, and consisted of an interrelated set of research questions and an approach for coordinating the school and household procedures required to address the questions. The research questions pertain to language minority children with limited English proficiency who are in need of special instructional services and are as follows:

● How many children are in need?

● How many children in need are being served?

● What types of educational needs do these children have?

The first question was the focus of the effort to count limited English proficient children in the household survey portion of the CESS. The second and third questions are the focus of the school survey. The third question was refined into three subquestions:

● How many children receive full service?

● How many children receive partial service?

● How many children receive no service?

Understanding the number of children who receive different levels of bilingual instruction and other services not only provides important information for Congressional deliberations about the scope of future legislation, but also supplies information for the Education Department to focus its future program efforts in bilingual education.

The approach used to address the research questions entailed coordinating definitions and procedures from two surveys: **the household survey,** designed to count the number of children in need, and **the pupil survey,** designed to determine the needs and services for limited English proficient students. Definitions of essential terms in both surveys were identical, particularly definitions of "language minority" and "limited English proficiency." Procedures in the two surveys were coordinated by performing the school survey with children identified in the household survey.

Specifications for the Pupil Survey Questionnaire

The pupil survey was designed to meet two purposes. The first was to obtain information on the nature of **instructional services** provided to limited English proficient children. The second was to identify the **educational needs** of limited English proficient children in comparison with language minority children who were more proficient in English. The CESS advisory group established complete specifications for design of the pupil services questionnaire (Appendix B) to meet both purposes.

Instructional Services. The pupil survey questionnaire was designed to determine both the type and level of instructional service. The **type of service** was determined from responses to questions about four instructional components: (1) English language instruction (including English language arts, English as a second language, and remedial English); (2) language arts in the non-English language; (3) content area instruction in the non-English language;

and (4) instruction related to the cultural background of the children. Each component is an essential element in the definition of bilingual education provided in the Bilingual Education Act. It was expected that students would receive these components singly or in combination. Instructional types were defined from different combinations of components and included the following:

- Bilingual bicultural instruction (English language instruction, either non-English language arts or non-English language content, or both, and instruction related to the cultural background of LEP pupils)

- Bilingual instruction (English language instruction, and either non-English language arts or non-English language content, or both)

- English as a second language (with or without instruction related to cultural background)

- English-medium instruction (either English language arts or remedial English, with or without instruction related to cultural background).

The **level of instructional service** to students was depicted according to three criteria applied to the instructional types. The criteria were established by a task force of the CESS advisory group as minimum requirements for instruction to meet the educational needs of limited English proficient children, and were as follows:

- Assessment of English language proficiency and, for bilingual instructional types, of proficiency in the non-English language

- Staffing by professionals in all instructional areas

- Instruction for at least 5 hours per week in English and, for bilingual instructional types, at least 5 hours per week in the non-English language.

The number of limited English proficient children receiving services in instructional types that meet the relevant criteria gives a preliminary picture of the ways in which combined Federal, State, and local efforts address the educational needs of language minority children.

Educational Needs. The CESS advisory group recommended using multiple indices of need to encompass the full range of difficulties limited English proficient children might experience. Included among the indices of needs were the following:

- Reading achievement

- Grade retention

- Overagedness in grade.

Additionally, information was requested on the procedures by which schools could identify whether language minority children were in need, and could monitor their progress through the school system. The information requested was of two types:

- School assessment to identify limited English proficiency among language minorities and, where available, the specific classification

- School assessment to monitor progress through the educational system in reading and subject areas for both English and non-English languages.

Pilot Study

The pupil survey questionnaire was pilot tested at three sites surrounding a major metropolitan area in the northeastern United States. The sites varied in concentration of language minority students and in size of schools. The questionnaire was mailed to sites after initial telephone contact with a coordinator in the local education agency, requesting completion of the questionnaire according to instructions provided. Recommendations for revisions of the instrument obtained in debriefing sessions with teachers and school coordinators were incorporated in final versions of the instrument.

Field Data Collection

Data collection with the pupil survey questionnaire was coordinated with the household survey in Spring 1978. A follow-up in Spring 1979 was performed on the pupil survey to increase the response rate. Pupil survey questionnaires were mailed to schools enrolling children in the 5–14 age range where cooperation had been obtained from parents and from State and local education agencies. As many as four call-backs were made with a local or State coordinator for the study to assure that questionnaires were returned completed.

Response Rates

Response rates for the school survey were determined for the following major subpopulations in the CESS: California, Texas, New York, and the remainder of the country combined. Results are shown in Table II–1, Response Rates by Subpopulation for the Parent Consent Form and Pupil Survey Questionnaire for Children Aged 5–14 Years.

The response rate nationally for the parent consent form (Appendix C) for releasing access to school information was 96%. That is, nearly all of the language minority parents with children in the study on whom school data would be collected gave their signed approval for gaining access to school records.

The response rate nationally for the pupil survey questionnaire was 54%. By subpopula-tion, the range was substantial and varied from 10% in Texas to 79% in the balance of the country excluding California and New York. The response rate in Texas was far too limited to justify including the data in analyses. To build a sufficient number of cases for analysis, data for California, New York, and the remainder of the country were combined. The overall response rate in these areas, once Texas had been removed from the analysis, was 97% for the parent consent form and 67% for the pupil survey questionnaire.

The low response rates for Texas and California were due mainly to the State procedures required to obtain permission to contact local school districts under the Committee on Education and Information System (CEIS) of the Council of Chief State School Officers. In California, notification of permission to approach local education agencies (LEAs) was not received until late in the school year. Thus, follow-up was limited by proximity to the end of the school year. In Texas, only 5 out of 21 school districts sampled in the State agreed to participate in the study in response to a mail request from the State Education Agency. Only those that agreed could be contacted directly by project personnel. Non-response adjustments were built into the survey weighting pro-

Table II–1

Response Rates by Subpopulation for the Parent Consent Form and the Pupil Survey Questionnaire for Children Aged 5–14 Years

Subpopulation	Eligible	Parent Consent Form		Pupil Survey Questionnaire	
	N	%	N	%	N
California	310	97%	301	38%	114
Texas	460	95%	437	10%	44
New York	279	98%	273	64%	175
Remainder	860	96%	826	79%	654
Total[1]	1909	96%	1833	54%	990

1. The Pupil Survey Questionnaire response rate not including Texas is 67%.

cedures, and are described in the CESS report on the count of limited English proficient children (O'Malley, 1981). Further comments on the response rates for California and Texas are given in Appendix A of this document.

Sources of Error

The particular sample used in the pupil survey is only one of all possible samples of the same size that could have been selected using this sample design from the population of language minorities. Because each of the possible samples is unique, estimates derived from the different samples would differ from each other and produce sampling error. Confidence intervals, which represent an index of the size of sampling error, were not computed for estimates based on the pupil survey because they would lend a false sense of security to data that contain other known sources of error. Further, though the sample was selected to be representative, low response rates may have introduced error or bias into the sample estimate in certain locations. (It could be argued that instructional approaches in Texas or California schools represent types of approaches which are underrepresented because of low response rates.) These low response rates in some cases may be responsible for low cell frequencies in data analyses. Thus, numbers associated with population estimates that are based on small samples are not presented in this report. Percentages are reported because errors associated with percentages tend to be lower than with the raw number they represent in the numerator of a proportion. Any attempt to generalize to the total population should be made with extreme caution.

III. RESULTS OF THE PUPIL SURVEY TO ESTIMATE EDUCATIONAL NEEDS OF AND SERVICES FOR LIMITED ENGLISH PROFICIENT CHILDREN

The type of instruction received by limited English proficient children has been a point of conjecture since the 1974 needs assessment was mandated in ESEA Title VII. Federal support for bilingual programs can be documented more readily than support from State and local sources. Yet the extent and source of support, even when support is available, offer no information about the type and level of services it provides.

The U.S. Office of Bilingual Education supported programs enrolling approximately 186 thousand children in Spring 1978 for California, New York, and the remainder of the country (excepting Texas), the geographic areas represented in the school data analysis for the CESS. The number of limited English proficient children enrolled in special programs of all types under State and local support has never been determined nationally. Further, the proportion of limited English proficient (LEP) to non-limited English proficient (NLEP) language minority children enrolled in programs funded from all sources has been subject to considerable speculation.

The results of the CESS provide only a preliminary picture of the type and level of services received by LEP children in three major geographic subpopulations: California, New York, and the remainder of the United States, excluding Texas. The picture received from this study should be considered preliminary for at least four reasons. First, children identified in the CESS on whom school information was received are different from children with no school information. Differences in basic sampling weights between children with and without school information were evident, particularly in California (Appendix A). The precise influence of this difference on school data is unknown in the absence of additional analyses of the CESS data, which were not possible for this report.

Second, variations in actual school practice may exist for similar patterns of responses to the survey questionnaire. Although the CESS was designed only to provide a general picture of these services, the potential variation in underlying services must be recognized. For example, schools reporting to have employed professional staff in implementing language arts in the students' non-English language could have retained either highly or minimally qualified staff by reason of training, experience, or language proficiency. A national survey of teachers providing instruction to limited English speaking students performed by the National Center for Education Statistics strongly indicates that only a small percentage of these teachers are trained for their task and possess the proficiency to use the student's non-English language in instruction (Waggoner, 1979). Responses to the CESS school questionnaire only indicate whether, from the school's point of view, the person who speaks to the child in English and non-English languages is professional or not. In a similar manner, schools reporting to have used the student's non-English language for, say, 10 clock hours per week may have used the language to only a limited degree for actual instruction and more for casual communication. One study, although on a limited sample, suggests that teachers overestimate both the extent of non-English language use in general and the extent to which the language is used in instruction, as contrasted with general directions or social dialogue (Bruck and Schultz, n.d.). As a final example, the survey questionnaire simply asked, "Does the student receive instruction on the culture or heritage associated with his or her non-English language background?" Schools reporting to have included culture in instruction could be doing nothing more than discussing foods or, on the other hand, could actually be adapting instructional strategies to the particular learning styles associated with a given cultural background.

A third, and perhaps most important, reason to term the study's picture preliminary is that services are examined for children identified as LEP and NLEP on the basis of the assessment administered as part of this study. The assessment procedures may or may not agree with those used by the schools participating in the study. School districts might not be providing special, language-related services because either the services were not available or the children were not considered to be eligible for them based on district assessment procedures. The CESS pupil survey data must be interpreted with respect to the language instrument administered to children in the CESS household sample and used for making LEP/NLEP distinctions. This points to the need for examining procedures used for identification, the difficulty in performing this type of study, and the need for further analysis of the data.

Finally, confidence intervals within which the estimates fall were not computed. Confidence intervals would indicate the range in which similar estimates based on the same sample size would fluctuate. However, providing confidence intervals would lend a false sense of security to the interpretation of numbers that should be considered tentative given the school survey response rates and potential variation in school practice for similar responses to the school questionnaire.

In sum, the CESS school data should be interpreted with caution. At best, the results provide an estimate for the type and level of school services offered to LEP children—but only for children in schools that elected to respond in three subpopulations: California, New York, and the remainder of the country except for Texas. As will be seen, the results nevertheless show an interesting pattern, and, it is hoped, will generate a paradigm for future investigations, in terms of both what the approach reveals as well as what it fails to disclose about the educational services provided to LEP students.

Results of the pupil survey are presented in four broad categories. The first includes a description of student enrollment by instructional types for LEP and NLEP children from Spanish and non-Spanish language minority backgrounds. The second category contains information on the grade distribution and the source of Federal, State, and local support received for different instructional types. The third category identifies and applies criteria for the quality or level for each major instructional type. In the final category are indices of educational need for LEP and NLEP students from Spanish and non-Spanish language minority backgrounds.

Student Enrollment by Instructional Type

Instructional types defined in the CESS included the following: Bilingual bicultural, Bilingual, English as a second language (ESL), and English language instruction (ELI). All bilingual instruction contained some form of English language instruction, possibly ESL or other variations such as English language arts and remedial instruction in English. Both ESL and ELI represent program approaches that with some children contained a cultural component, but with others was provided without cultural emphasis. ESL could have been accompanied by an English language arts component or remedial instruction in English, whereas ELI included either of these but no ESL. An "other" category was provided for all programs that did not fit one of the specified types.

For each instructional type, CESS task force requirements for level of service were applied. The criteria were requirements, in the judgment of the task force, for a program type to be offered at a minimally acceptable level of quality and are discussed in detail in Appendix A. The criteria were as follows:

- Language assessment in English and, for bilingual instruction, in non-English languages

- Fully professional staffing in all instruction

- A minimum of 5 hours per week in English and, for bilingual instruction, 5 hours per week in non-English language instruction.

Preliminary analyses revealed that less than 1% of the limited English proficient children aged 5–14 years received bilingual instructional types to a level acceptable to the task force (Miranda, 1979b). These results were based on analyses of data obtained from New York and the remainder of the country, excluding California and Texas. The percentage of limited English proficient children receiving bilingual instruction at a level acceptable to the task force was far smaller than had been anticipated. Because the percentage was so small, data analyses planned for identifying variables associated with bilingual service provision had to be altered.

Table III–1

Estimated Number of Language Minority Children, Aged 5–14 Years, by Language Background, English Proficiency, and Type of Instruction in the United States: Spring 1978 (Numbers in 000)[a]

Program Type		Total			Spanish			Non-Spanish		
		Total	Proficiency		Total	Proficiency		Total	Proficiency	
			LEP	NLEP		LEP	NLEP		LEP	NLEP
Bilingual Bicultural	n	362	297	64	318	275	43	43	22	21
	%	12%	17%	5%	19%	23%	8%	3%	4%	2%
Bilingual	n	131	108	23	90	79	11	41	29	12
	%	4%	6%	2%	5%	7%	2%	3%	5%	1%
ESL	n	229	189	40	135	119	15	95	70	25
	%	7%	11%	3%	8%	10%	3%	7%	13%	3%
English Language Medium	n	2,149	1,003	1,146	1,014	604	410	1,135	400	735
	%	69%	58%	83%	60%	51%	81%	80%	73%	85%
Other	n	226	124	102	124	98	27	101	26	75
	%	7%	7%	7%	7%	8%	5%	7%	5%	9%
Total	n	3,097	1,723	1,375	1,681	1,175	507	1,416	548	858

a. Totals may not add due to rounding. Regions include California, New York, and the remainder of the country except for Texas.

Subsequent data analyses were designed to reveal the number of children aged 5–14 years receiving alternative types of instruction independent of the task force requirements. Each task force criterion for level of service was then applied to determine which of the criteria were not met. All analyses include California, New York, and the remainder of the country except Texas. Table III–1 presents the percentages of limited English proficient (LEP) and non-limited English proficient (NLEP) children receiving different forms of instruction.

Special instructional services for LEP children were shown to vary considerably when task force requirements for level of service were removed. An estimated 297 thousand, or 17% of all LEP children, received instruction in one or more courses through a non-English language accompanied by a cultural component (bilingual bicultural type). An additional 108 thousand, or 6% of all LEP children, received this form of instruction without culture (bilingual type). An estimated 189 thousand, or 11% of all LEP children, received ESL, whereas 1 million, or 58%, received an all-English instructional program without ESL.

For the different language groups, roughly 30% of the Spanish language LEP children received either bilingual bicultural or bilingual instruction, and 10% of the Spanish language LEP children were in ESL. Just more than 50% of the Spanish language minority LEP children received standard English-medium instruction, compared with 73% of the non-Spanish language minority LEP students. The small percentage of children in the "other" category indicates that most instruction in which both LEP and NLEP children were enrolled could be classified with the typology used.

The extent to which targeted bilingual and ESL services reach LEP, as contrasted with NLEP, children **can be constructed from** Table III–1. Of the language minority children who received either bilingual bicultural or bilingual instruction, 406 out of 493 thousand, or 82%, were LEP, while only roughly 87 thousand, or 18%, were NLEP. Of those who received ESL, 189 out of 229 thousand, or 83%, were LEP compared with 17% NLEP. When neither bilingual instruction nor ESL was available, as with English-medium instruction,

services were roughly evenly divided between LEP and NLEP students. Approximately 1 million, or 47%, of all language minority children receiving standard English-medium instruction were LEP.

Characteristics of Instructional Types

Grade level and sources of support for programs enrolling LEP children are two major characteristics about which little has been known. Conventional wisdom and some data from State and Federal sources suggest that most bilingual instruction occurs at the elementary level. Information is virtually nonexistent about local support for bilingual or other instruction offered to LEP children. In Table III–2 and subsequent tables, in order to build sufficient cases for analysis, children receiving all bilingual types of instruction were combined, as were those receiving all types of English language instruction.

Grade Distribution. By far the majority of children aged 5–14 receiving bilingual instruction were concentrated in grades K–6, as shown in Table III–2, Estimated Number of Language Minority Children, Aged 5–14 Years, by Type of Instruction, English Proficiency, and Grade Level in the United States: Spring 1978. The greater concentration in lower grades is consistent for both LEP and NLEP children. LEP children enrolled in English instruction are also concentrated in lower grades. However, NLEP children in English programs are more evenly distributed across the grades.

Source of Support. Federal support for children receiving bilingual instruction comes from a variety of sources, as shown in Table III–3, Estimated Number of Language Minority Children, Aged 5–14 Years, by Type of Instruction, English Proficiency, and Source of Federal Support. The results in Table III–3 show four different sources of Federal support: ESEA Title I (Compensatory Education), ESEA Title I Migrant Education, ESEA Title VII (Bilingual Education), and ESAA Title VII (Assistance for Desegregating Schools). Although each source of funding shown is presented independently, it is expected that some of the children are recipients of multiple fund-

Table III–2

Estimated Number of Language Minority Children, Aged 5–14 Years, by Type of Instruction, English Proficiency, and Grade Level in the United States: Spring 1978 (Numbers in 000)[a]

Grade Level		Total			Bilingual			English			Other		
			Proficiency			Proficiency			Proficiency			Proficiency	
		Total	LEP	NLEP	Total	LEP	NLEP	Total	LEP	NLEP	Total	LEP	NLEP
K–3	n	1,368	851	517	275	217	58	1,008	585	423	86	49	37
	%	44%	49%	38%	58%	54%	66%	42%	49%	36%	36%	39%	36%
4–6	n	950	471	479	144	118	26	760	323	438	46	30	16
	%	31%	27%	35%	29%	29%	29%	32%	27%	37%	21%	24%	16%
7–9	n	718	372	347	74	70	4	567	259	308	78	43	35
	%	23%	22%	25%	15%	17%	5%	24%	22%	26%	34%	34%	34%
Not Reported	n	60	29	31	b	b	b	44	26	18	16	2	14
	%	2%	2%	2%	0%	0%	0%	2%	2%	1%	7%	2%	13%
Total	n	3,097	1,723	1,375	493	406	87	2,378	1,193	1,186	226	124	102

a. Totals may not add due to rounding. Regions include California, New York, and the remainder of the country except for Texas.
b. Fewer than one thousand.

ing categories. Schools could have indicated other sources of support on the pupil questionnaire, such as Follow Through or Right to Read, but only in the four categories shown was the incidence sufficient to warrant reporting the results.

In addition, it should be pointed out that the percentages reported in Table III–3 reflect the types of services received by language minority children identified as LEP and NLEP according to the study's criteria. The criteria for identifying LEP students do not necessarily always agree with local criteria for identification. This means that certain students may not have been identified as LEP and NLEP according to the schools' criteria and thus were not targeted for particular types of services. The data must be interpreted with this caveat in mind.

The type of support received by LEP students varied, depending on the type of classroom instruction. Of LEP children receiving bilingual instruction, 27% received funding from ESEA Title I; 4%, from Title I Migrant Education; 18%, from ESEA Title VII; and 4%, from ESAA Title VII. For LEP children in English language programs, 23% received funding from ESEA Title I; 3%, from Title I Migrant Education; 4%, from ESEA Title VII; and 2%, from ESAA Title VII. Across all types of instruction, ESEA Title VII support was received by an estimated 7% of all LEP students. These percentages should be interpreted in light of the relative numbers of LEP students estimated to be enrolled in each instructional type. The number of students in English-medium instruction is much larger. Total LEP enrollment in all bilingual instruction was 406 thousand, compared with 1.2 million in English-medium instruction and 124 thousand in "other" instruction.

Table III–3 can also be used **to construct** the number and percentage of students receiving a particular type of instruction for a given funding source. Of the 417 thousand LEP students receiving support from ESEA Title I, 273 thousand, or 65%, were in English-medium instruction, 26% were in bilingual instruction, and 9% received "other" instructional types. Of the 76 thousand LEP students receiving

support from ESEA Title I, Migrant Education, 16 thousand or 21% were in bilingual instruction, 41% were in English-medium instruction, and 38% were in other types of instruction. Of the 37 thousand LEP children receiving ESAA Title VII support, 46% received bilingual instruction, 54% received English-medium instruction, and a negligible percent received "other" forms of instruction.

Of the 126 thousand LEP children receiving support from ESEA Title VII, the Federal bilingual program, an estimated 58% were in bilingual instruction; 40%, in English medium instruction; and 3%, in "other" forms of instruction. Overall, of the 173 thousand language minority children receiving ESEA Title VII support, an estimated 105 thousand, or 61%, received support for bilingual instruction, as contrasted with 64 thousand, or 37%, who received ESEA Title VII support in an English language program. While this appears to indicate that not all ESEA Title VII support was expended for bilingual instruction, it may simply represent differences between identification procedures used in this study and those used by the school district.

If one discounts the type of instructional support and keeps in mind the differences in identification criteria, targeted Federal support for LEP students compared with potentially misdirected resources for NLEP language minority children **can be constructed** from Table III–3. For example, LEP students represent between 66% and 82% of all language minority children (compared with 18% and 34% NLEP) receiving Federal support. The estimated figures for each funding source are as follows: ESEA Title I, 417 thousand, or 79%, LEP students out of 529 thousand language minority recipients; ESEA Title I Migrant, 76 thousand, or 66%, LEP students out of 116 thousand language minority recipients; ESEA Title VII, 126 thousand, or 73%, LEP students out of 173 thousand language minority recipients; and ESAA Title VII, 37 thousand, or 82%, LEP students out of 45 thousand language minority students. In general, it appears that the majority of Federal resources are targeted to LEP students, with the remainder going to NLEP language minority students who may meet other Federal eligibility requirements.

Table III-3

Estimated Number of Language Minority Children, Aged 5–14 Years, by Type of Instruction, English Proficiency, and Source of Federal Support in the United States: Spring 1978 (Numbers in 000)[a]

Source of Support		Total			Bilingual Instruction			English Medium Instruction			Other		
		Total	Proficiency		Total	Proficiency		Total	Proficiency		Total	Proficiency	
			LEP	NLEP		LEP	NLEP		LEP	NLEP		LEP	NLEP
Title I	n	529	417	112	111	108	3	346	273	74	72	37	36
	%	17%	79%	8%	23%	26%	4%	15%	65%	6%	32%	29%	35%
Title I Migrant	n	116	76	40	22	16	6	36	31	5	58	29	29
	%	4%	66%	3%	5%	4%	7%	2%	3%	0%	2%	23%	28%
ESEA Title VII	n	173	126	46	105	73	31	64	50	14	4	4	0
	%	6%	73%	3%	61%	58%	36%	37%	40%	1%	2%	3%	0%
ESAA Title VII (Desegregation)	n	45	37	8	17	17	b	28	20	8	b	b	b
	%	1%	82%	1%	3%	46%	0%	1%	54%	1%	0%	0%	0%
Total	n	3,097	1,723	1,375	493	406	87	2,378	1,193	1,186	226	124	102

a. Estimated numbers may not add up to total because of overlapping sources of support. Regions include California, New York, and the remainder of the country except for Texas.

b. Sample size too small to report. Fewer than one thousand.

Table III–4

Estimated Number of Language Minority Children, Aged 5–14 Years, by Type of Instruction, English Proficiency, and Non-Federal Source of Support in the United States: Spring 1978 (Numbers in 000)[a]

Source of Support		Total	Proficiency		Bilingual Instruction	Proficiency		English Medium Instruction	Proficiency		Other	Proficiency	
		Total	LEP	NLEP	Total	LEP	NLEP	Total	LEP	NLEP	Total	LEP	NLEP
State Bilingual	n	330	248	82	161	147	14	128	90	38	41	12	29
	%	11%	14%	6%	33%	36%	16%	5%	8%	3%	18%	10%	28%
Other State	n	297	204	93	56	55	1	226	147	79	14	1	13
	%	10%	12%	7%	11%	14%	1%	10%	12%	7%	6%	1%	13%
Local Bilingual	n	296	225	71	209	169	39	87	56	b	b	b	b
	%	10%	13%	5%	42%	42%	45%	4%	5%	3%	0%	0%	0%
Total	n	3,097	1,723	1,375	493	406	87	2,378	1,193	1,186	226	124	102

a. Estimated numbers may not add up to total because of overlap among sources of support. Regions include California, New York, and the remainder of the country except for Texas.

b. Sample size too small to report. Fewer than one thousand.

Finally, the number of children estimated to receive ESEA Title VII support by the CESS and by the U.S. Office of Education's (USOE) Office of Bilingual Education can be compared. In the CESS, an estimated 173 thousand LEP and NLEP children were enrolled in classrooms of all types that were reported by schools to have received assistance from ESEA Title VII. These children were all aged 5–14 years in Spring 1978 and were from language minority backgrounds residing in the three areas for which CESS school data were reported: California, New York, and the remainder of the U.S. excepting Texas. USOE reported that an estimated 186 thousand children were enrolled in programs receiving ESEA Title VII funds in Spring 1978 in the same geographic areas. USOE's figures were obtained from grant proposals submitted at the beginning of the academic year 1977–78.

USOE's figures for ESEA Title VII enrollments are remarkably close to the CESS estimates. The slight discrepancy could stem from a number of sources. The direction of the discrepancy can be anticipated only for the first two of these sources. First, age differences between the CESS and USOE groups could produce a larger figure for USOE's estimated enrollments in ESEA Title VII programs. Although concentrated in the 5–14 age range, as were the CESS children, ESEA Title VII programs extend throughout secondary school. Second, enrollments in ESEA Title VII most likely include English language background students, as required by law, thereby producing a larger figure for USOE's estimate. Third, the USOE figures were collected before the beginning of the school year, whereas the CESS figures were obtained in Spring 1978; enrollments could have changed over that duration. The final potential sources of difference are the CESS sampling error and the non-response rate. In any case, the discrepancy is very small.

Non-Federal sources of support are shown in Table III–4, Estimated Number of Language Minority Children, Aged 5–14 Years, by Type of Instruction, English Proficiency, and Non-Federal Source of Support. Of LEP children receiving bilingual instruction, 36% received State bilingual support and 42% received local bilingual support, whereas only 14% received other State support. State and local support for children in bilingual instruction clearly was more prevalent than any source of Federal support. Potential overlap between sources of support was not analyzed. For LEP children enrolled in English language programs, only a very small percentage received special support from either State or local funding.

Levels of Instruction

The CESS task force for program types and levels of service identified a series of criteria that are required, in their judgment, for bilingual and English language instruction to be delivered acceptably. The criteria, as noted earlier, dealt with three issues: (1) hours of instruction in English and non-English languages; (2) staffing by professionals rather than non-professionals; and (3) assessments of both English and non-English language proficiency.

Hours of Instruction. The CESS task force required acceptable bilingual instruction to include at least 5 hours of English language instruction and 5 hours of non-English language instruction per week. The results are shown in Table III–5, Estimated Number of Language Minority Children, Aged 5–14 Years, by Type of Instruction, English Proficiency, and Clock Hours of Instruction in English and Non-English Languages per Week.

Inspection of Table III–5 indicates that the percentage of LEP children for whom the task force criteria on hours of language instruction were met depended on both the language and the type of instruction. Criteria for English language instruction tended to be met in both bilingual and English-medium instruction. Five or more hours of instruction in English per week (constructed from information provided) were given to an estimated 83% of the LEP students in bilingual instruction, and to 76% of the LEP students in English-medium instruction, but to only 35% of the LEP students in other forms of instruction. The clock hours specified for English include only English language arts (ELA), English as a second language (ESL), and remedial or corrective instruction in English (RCE). In contrast, clock hours specified for non-English languages include language arts, content areas, history and culture, and other subjects.

Table III-5

Estimated Number of Language Minority Children, Aged 5–14, by Type of Instruction, English Proficiency, and Clock Hours of Instruction in English and Non-English Languages per Week in the United States: Spring 1978 (Numbers in 000)[a]

Language of Instruction	Hours		Total			Bilingual Instruction			English Medium Instruction			Other		
				Proficiency			Proficiency			Proficiency			Proficiency	
			Total	LEP	NLEP	Total	LEP	NLEP	Total	LEP	NLEP	Total	LEP	NLEP
English	0–4	n	638	275	363	94	55	39	540	216	324	4	4	b
		%	21%	16%	26%	19%	14%	45%	23%	18%	27%	2%	3%	0%
	5–9	n	1,060	511	549	154	142	12	873	336	537	34	34	b
		%	34%	30%	40%	31%	35%	14%	37%	28%	45%	15%	27%	0%
	10+	n	1,096	775	321	228	196	b	858	569	288	11	10	1
		%	35%	45%	23%	46%	48%	37%	36%	48%	24%	5%	8%	1%
	Not Reported	n	303	162	141	17	13	4	108	72	36	178	77	101
		%	10%	9%	10%	3%	3%	4%	5%	6%	3%	79%	62%	99%
	Total	n	3,097	1,723	1,375	493	406	87	2,378	1,193	1,186	226	124	102
Non-English	0–4	n	2,743	1,427	1,316	154	117	38	2,371	1,193	1,178	218	118	100
		%	88%	83%	96%	31%	29%	43%	97%	100%	99%	96%	95%	96%
	5–9	n	149	121	28	145	118	26	b	b	b	4	3	b
		%	5%	7%	2%	29%	29%	30%	0%	0%	0%	2%	2%	1%
	10+	n	205	174	31	193	170	b	b	b	b	b	b	b
		%	7%	10%	2%	39%	42%	26%	0%	0%	1%	2%	3%	0%
	Not Reported	n	3	b	3	b	b	b	b	b	b	3	b	3
		%	3%	0%	0%	0%	0%	0%	0%	0%	0%	0%	0%	3%
	Total	n	3,097	1,723	1,375	493	406	87	2,378	1,193	1,186	226	124	102

a. Estimated numbers may not add up to total because of rounding. Regions include California, New York, and the remainder of the country except for Texas.

b. Sample size too small to report. Fewer than one thousand.

Task force requirements in non-English languages tended to be met in bilingual instruction at rates only slightly below the level of requirements for English language instruction. An estimated 71% of the students in bilingual instruction were taught in a non-English language for 5 hours or more per week. The percentage of students taught 5 hours or more per week in non-English languages for other instructional types was 4%, and for what was reported to be English-medium instruction, an estimated 8%. Further analysis indicated that the 8% was generally associated with English instruction that was accompanied by cultural instruction, whether it was English as a second language or English language arts.

Of all LEP language minority students, the percentage receiving bilingual instruction consistent with the task force recommendations for minimum quality **can be constructed** from further analysis of the data underlying Table III–1 and Table III–5. An estimated 406 thousand, or 23%, of all 1.7 million LEP language minority children received bilingual instruction, as noted in Table III–1. Roughly 289 thousand, or 71%, of these 406 thousand LEP children receiving bilingual instruction were taught in non-English languages at least 5 hours per week, as shown in Table III–5. The figure 289 thousand represents approximately 17% of the total 1.7 million LEP language minority children. Thus, based on this task force criterion, an estimated 17% of all language minority children in need, those who are LEP, received bilingual instruction that could be considered acceptable.

Students who were not receiving bilingual instruction could nevertheless be receiving instruction in an English-medium environment that meets other task force criteria. An estimated 1.2 million, or 69%, of the 1.7 million LEP students were receiving English-medium instruction, as noted in Table III–1. Applying the task force criteria for hours per week in English to English-medium instruction, as was performed above, 76% or about 905 thousand of the 1.2 million LEP students in English-medium instruction were taught at least 5 hours per week in English. The figure 905 thousand represents approximately 53% of the total 1.7 mil-

lion LEP language minority children. Therefore, based only on the criterion concerned with hours of instruction in English for a student in English-medium instruction, roughly two out of three LEP children were receiving instruction consistent with the task force recommendations in this area.

Staffing. The task force recommended that all instructional staff should be professional irrespective of the language, component, or program type. Neither paraprofessionals nor volunteers were an acceptable substitute for a staff considered to be qualified by school district standards for professional status. The results of analyses for staffing are shown in Table III–6, Estimated Number of Language Minority Children, Aged 5–14 Years, by Type of Instruction, English Proficiency, Staffing, and Language of Instruction.

Task force criteria for staffing were generally met irrespective of student language background for the two major instructional types. An estimated 98% or more of the LEP children in bilingual and English-medium instruction were taught in English by persons the school designated to be professional. However, for "other types" of instruction, 57% of the LEP students were taught in English by a professional. In non-English languages, a professional taught 93% of the LEP children in bilingual instruction. As indicated earlier, staff designated as professional by the school may not have been trained or experienced in bilingual instruction or in other areas where they were expected to offer services to limited English proficient children.

The level of educational service provided to LEP students **can be constructed** based on assumptions made about appropriate instruction in the light of the task force criteria. If bilingual instruction with professionals teaching non-English languages is the minimum accepted, the percentage of LEP students estimated to receive acceptable service is 23% or 402 thousand out of the total 1.7 million LEP children. On the other hand, if English-medium instruction by professionals is the only condition required, an estimated 96%, or 1.6 out of 1.7 million, LEP children received acceptable service.

Table III-6

Estimated Number of Language Minority Children, Aged 5–14 Years, by Type of Instruction, English Proficiency, Staffing, and Language of Instruction in the United States: Spring 1978 (Numbers in 000)[a]

Language of Instruction	Staffing		Total			Bilingual Instruction			English Medium Instruction			Other		
			Total	Proficiency LEP	Proficiency NLEP	Total	Proficiency LEP	Proficiency NLEP	Total	Proficiency LEP	Proficiency NLEP	Total	Proficiency LEP	Proficiency NLEP
English	Professional	n	2,923	1,647	1,276	489	402	87	2,350	1,174	1,176	84	71	13
		%	94%	96%	93%	99%	99%	100%	99%	98%	99%	37%	57%	12%
	Non-Professional	n	174	76	98	4	4	b	28	19	9	142	53	89
		%	6%	4%	7%	1%	1%	0%	1%	2%	1%	63%	43%	88%
	Not Reported	n	b	b	b	b	b	b	b	b	b	b	b	b
		%	0%	0%	0%	0%	0%	0%	0%	0%	0%	0%	0%	0%
	Total	n	3,097	1,723	1,375	493	406	87	2,378	1,193	1,186	226	124	102
Non-English	Professional	n	486	402	84	450	379	71	19	8	11	17	15	2
		%	16%	23%	6%	91%	93%	81%	1%	1%	1%	8%	12%	2%
	Non-professional	n	1,284	677	606	43	27	16	1,214	1624	1590	26	26	b
		%	41%	39%	44%	9%	7%	19%	51%	52%	49%	12%	21%	0%
	Not Reported	n	1,328	644	684	b	b	b	1,146	561	585	182	83	99
		%	43%	37%	50%	0%	0%	0%	48%	47%	49%	81%	67%	98%
	Total	n	3,097	1,723	1,375	493	406	87	2,378	1,193	1,186	226	124	102

a. Estimated numbers may not add up to the total because of rounding. Regions include California, New York, and the remainder of the country except for Texas.

b. Sample size too small to report. Fewer than one thousand.

Table III–7

Estimated Number of Language Minority Children, Aged 5–14 Years, by Type of Instruction, English Proficiency, and Language Proficiency Assessment in the United States: Spring 1978 (Numbers in 000)[a]

Type of Test		Total			Bilingual Instruction			English Medium Instruction			Other		
			Proficiency			Proficiency			Proficiency			Proficiency	
		Total	LEP	NLEP	Total	LEP	NLEP	Total	LEP	NLEP	Total	LEP	NLEP
English Language	n	926	591	335	221	174	47	683	401	282	22	16	6
	%	30%	34%	24%	44%	43%	50%	29%	34%	24%	10%	13%	6%
Non-English Languages	n	424	271	153	118	97	21	276	156	120	31	18	13
	%	14%	16%	11%	24%	24%	24%	12%	13%	10%	14%	14%	13%
Total	n	3,097	1,723	1,375	493	406	87	2,378	1,193	1,186	226	124	102

a. Numbers may not add up to total because of rounding and overlapping categories. Regions include California, New York, and the remainder of the country except for Texas.

b. Sample size too small to report. Fewer than one thousand.

Language Assessment. One major purpose of English language assessment among language minority students is to identify students who can profit from instruction in English. Similarly, assessment in the non-English language helps the school to determine the student's capability to perform in a non-English instructional medium. The task force recommended the use of standardized tests in both English and non-English languages in bilingual instruction. Only English language standardized tests were required in English language instruction. The results of questions posed to schools about language assessment are presented in Table III–7, Estimated Number of Language Minority Students, Aged 5–14 Years, by Type of Instruction, English Proficiency, and Language Proficiency Assessment.

Three principal findings are evident from inspecting the results presented in Table III–7. First, task force requirements for language proficiency assessment tended to be met more for English language assessment than for non-English language assessment in the two major instructional types. Tests to assess English language proficiency in the context of bilingual instruction were administered in English to 44% of the language minority children, but were administered in non-English languages to 24% of the language minority children. In the context of English language instruction, English language proficiency was assessed for 29% of the language minority students, and non-English language proficiency was assessed for 12% of these students.

A second finding was that task force requirements for language proficiency assessment tended to be met more in bilingual instruction than in English-medium instruction. Using some of these same percentages, tests of English language proficiency were administered to 44% of the language minority children in bilingual instruction, to 29% of the children in English-medium instruction, and to 10% of the children receiving other forms of instruction. Tests of non-English proficiency were administered to 24% of the students in bilingual instruction, to 12% of the students in English-medium instruction, and to 14% of the students in other instructional types.

The third finding is that application of the task force criteria for language assessment in bilingual instruction seriously diminished the percentage of LEP children being adequately served. Whereas 406 thousand, or 23%, of the 1.7 million LEP children received bilingual instruction overall, as shown in Table III-1 only 174 thousand, or 10%, of these 1.7 million received English language assessment and 97 thousand, or 6%, received non-English language assessment in the context of bilingual instruction.

Assuming that alternatives to bilingual instruction might meet the needs of LEP students and that assessment criteria are met yields a somewhat improved impression of services provided to LEP children. Of 1.7 million LEP children receiving all forms of instruction, 591 thousand, or 34%, received English language assessment, and 271 thousand, or 16%, received assessment in non-English languages.

Indices of Educational Need

The CESS advisory group was concerned with a variety of indices of educational need for LEP children. The prevailing impression was that multiple indicators of need were required to capture the range of additional services appropriate for these children beyond those used to describe the type and level of instructional programs. Of particular interest were indices reflecting needs of LEP, as contrasted with NLEP, children from Spanish and non–Spanish language minority backgrounds. The indices reported are as follows:

- Types of subject areas assessment received
- School language classification
- Reading achievement
- Grade retention
- Overagedness in grade.

Information on the first two indices is reported to reflect the school's capability to identify the children's educational needs, and the last three indices reflect the children's attainments in school.

Table III–8

Estimated Number of Language Minority Children, Aged 5–14 years, by Language Background, English Proficiency, and English Language Subject Area Assessments in the United States: Spring 1978
(Numbers in 000)[a]

English Language Assessment Instrument		Total			Spanish			Non-Spanish		
			Proficiency			Proficiency			Proficiency	
		Total	LEP	NLEP	Total	LEP	NLEP	Total	LEP	NLEP
Reading	n	1,881	1,071	810	1,084	772	313	796	299	497
	%	61%	62%	59%	65%	66%	62%	56%	55%	57%
Math	n	1,778	974	804	998	686	313	779	288	491
	%	57%	57%	58%	59%	58%	62%	55%	53%	57%
Other	n	886	422	464	450	283	167	436	139	296
	%	29%	25%	34%	27%	24%	33%	31%	25%	34%
Total	n	3,097	1,723	1,375	1,681	1,175	507	1,416	548	868

a. Numbers may not total due to rounding and to overlapping categories. Regions include California, New York, and the remainder of the country except for Texas.

Subject Area Assessment. Assessment of subject areas in both English and non-English languages enables schools to monitor the progress of children as they advance through the grades. Specific areas in which schools were requested to indicate subject area assessment included reading, math, and a combined category for other areas the schools were free to designate. The results for English language assessments are presented in Table III–8, Estimated Number of Language Minority Children, Aged 5–14 Years, by Language Background, English Proficiency, and English Language Subject Area Assessments.

Well over half the total number of LEP children received assessments administered to determine their English reading proficiency. An estimated 1.1 million, or 62%, of the 1.7 million LEP children for all languages combined received assessments in English reading. Assessments in math administered in English were provided to 57% of the LEP children and assessments in other areas were provided to 25%. Spanish language background students received English language subject area assessments at roughly the same level as students from non-Spanish language minority backgrounds. However, there was a modest tendency for English reading assessment instruments to be administered to more Spanish language background students than non-Spanish language minority students.

Non-English language subject area assessments were administered to LEP students less frequently than assessments in English in the same subject areas. The results for non-English language instruments are shown in Table III–9, Estimated Number of Language Minority Students, Aged 5–14 Years, by Language Background, English Proficiency, and Non-English Language Subject Area Assessments. An estimated 89 thousand, or only 5%, of the 1.7 million LEP children for all languages combined received subject area assessments in reading in their non-English language. The figures are roughly comparable for assessments administered in math and other areas in non-English languages, and differ little depending on the language background of the child.

School Classification. Classification of language minority children based on language proficiency in English is critical to providing instructional services addressed to their educational needs. Schools were requested in the CESS to indicate the English language proficiency of children in one of six categories: severely limited proficiency, very limited, slightly limited, adequate, can use English very well, and other.

Before discussing the school classifications, it should be noted that disagreement between the CESS classification of LEP and the school classification can be expected. The CESS classification of LEP was based on an assessment instrument that was grounded in acceptable school assessment practice observed onsite in field tests of the instrument. The school classification of LEP was based on a variety of procedures, only 34% of which involved proficiency assessment, as noted in Table III–7. The basis for the remaining classifications varied, but included teacher observation and locally developed tests. The school classification can be taken as an indication of the extent to which schools were able to recognize a need for special instructional services appropriate to the language needs of the children, given that the CESS test instrument is the valid criterion. The results are presented in Table III–10, Estimated Number of Language Minority Children, Aged 5–14 Years, by Language Background, English Proficiency, and School Classification.

The results suggest that schools tend to overrate the English language proficiency of language minority students, compared with results determined from the CESS test criterion. An estimated 385 thousand, or 22%, of the 1.7 million LEP students for all languages combined were rated by schools as able to use English very well, and 362 thousand, or 19%, of the total LEP children were rated as able to use English adequately. For 582 thousand, or 34%, of the total LEP students, the schools gave no response to the question about language proficiency. These figures differed little for children from Spanish and non-Spanish language backgrounds, except that the item non-response rate was higher for non-Spanish language minority students. Generally, the schools rated very few NLEP children in lower English language proficiency categories. The major concerns in school classification appear

Table III–9

Estimated Number of Language Minority Children, Aged 5–14 Years, by Language Background, English Proficiency, and Non-English Language Subject Area Assessments in the United States: Spring 1978 (Numbers in 000)[a]

Non-English Language Assessment Instrument		Total			Spanish			Non-Spanish		
			Proficiency			Proficiency			Proficiency	
		Total	LEP	NLEP	Total	LEP	NLEP	Total	LEP	NLEP
Reading	n	112	89	22	101	80	21	11	9	1
	%	4%	5%	2%	6%	7%	4%	1%	2%	0%
Math	n	68	48	20	66	47	19	3	1	1
	%	2%	3%	1%	4%	4%	4%	0%	0%	0%
Other	n	100	89	11	88	79	10	12	11	2
	%	3%	5%	1%	5%	7%	2%	1%	2%	0%
Total	n	3,097	1,723	1,375	1,681	1,175	507	1,416	548	868

a. Numbers may not total due to rounding and to overlapping categories. Regions include California, New York, and the remainder of the country except for Texas.

Table III-10

Estimated Number of Language Minority Children, Aged 5-14 Years, by Language Background, English Proficiency, and School Classification in the United States: Spring 1978 (Numbers in 000)[a]

School Classification		Total	Proficiency		Spanish	Proficiency		Non-Spanish	Proficiency	
		Total	LEP	NLEP	Total	LEP	NLEP	Total	LEP	NLEP
Severely Limited	n	59	53	6	45	45	b	14	8	6
	%	2%	3%	0%	3%	4%	0%	1%	1%	1%
Very Limited	n	149	126	23	103	84	19	47	43	4
	%	5%	7%	2%	6%	7%	4%	3%	8%	0%
Slightly Limited	n	277	242	35	227	200	27	50	42	8
	%	9%	14%	3%	14%	17%	5%	4%	8%	1%
Adequate	n	408	326	82	292	236	55	117	90	27
	%	13%	19%	6%	17%	20%	11%	8%	16%	3%
Can Use Very Well	n	877	385	492	538	323	215	339	62	277
	%	28%	22%	36%	32%	27%	42%	24%	11%	32%
Other	n	11	8	3	6	6	b	5	2	3
	%	0%	0%	0%	0%	0%	0%	0%	0%	0%
No Response	n	1,316	582	734	471	282	190	844	301	544
	%	42%	34%	53%	28%	24%	37%	60%	55%	63%
Total	n	3,097	1,723	1,375	1,681	1,175	507	1,416	548	868

a. Numbers may not total due to rounding. Regions include California, New York, and the remainder of the country except for Texas.

b. Sample size too small to report. Fewer than one thousand.

to be under-identification of children in need—that is, when compared with the procedures in this study—and failure to identify language classification at all. There does not appear to be any pervasive misclassification of NLEP children whose educational needs should be no different from native speakers of English.

Reading Achievement. School ratings of English reading achievement indicate whether students are perceived to be performing at or below grade level. Schools in the CESS were requested to rate the reading achievement of students in one of five categories: one-half year or more above grade level, at or close to grade level, one-half year or more below grade level, at or close to one full year below grade level, and more than one full year below grade level. Schools were requested to perform the ratings regardless of the information on which the rating was based. The results are presented in Table III–11, Estimated Number of Language Minority Children, Aged 5–14 Years, by Language Background, English Proficiency, and Reading Achievement.

The results suggest that a substantial percentage of LEP children are performing below grade level in English reading relative to NLEP children. Out of a total 1.7 million LEP children across all languages, an estimated 282 thousand, or 16%, were rated one-half to one year below grade level in reading; 216 thousand, or 13%, were rated at or close to one full year below grade level; and 393 thousand, or 23%, were rated more than one full year below grade level or less. Thus, 52% of the LEP children were rated one-half year or more below grade level. These figures did not differ appreciably for Spanish compared with non-Spanish language background students. The overall non-response rate for LEP students was only 13%. Thus, by some combination of information, schools generally were able to assign children to these English language reading achievement categories, even though only 62% of the LEP children overall were administered tests of their English reading proficiency, as noted in Table III-8.

Grade Retention and Overagedness in Grade. Failure of students to progress reg-ularly through the educational system, as suggested by grade retention and overagedness in grade, are strong indicators that students encounter severe difficulties in instruction. In the CESS, schools were requested to indicate whether students had been retained in grade by placing the student in one of four categories: repeated at least one grade or course, repeated part of a grade, never repeated, and no record. Children were considered overaged for grade if they were more than 2 years older than the age expected for their grade level. A difference of 2 years rather than 1 year was used because the data were collected in Spring 1978, and children may have passed a birthday from the date of enrollment at the beginning of the school year. The age expected for the grade was equivalent to the grade level plus 5 years. Results are presented in Table III–12, Estimated Number of Language Minority Children, Aged 5–14 Years, by Language Background, English Proficiency, Grade Retention, and Overagedness in Grade.

Results indicate that LEP students, in comparison with NLEP students, are subject to both more grade repetition and overagedness in grade. An estimated 189 thousand, or roughly 11%, of 1.7 million LEP children across all language groups repeated at least one grade or course, whereas only 2% of 1.4 million NLEP children repeated at least one grade or course. Only a small percentage of the LEP children repeated part of a grade. The nonresponse rate was 19%. The figures for the different language groups were roughly comparable, although relatively more Spanish language students than those of non-Spanish language minorities repeated at least one grade or course.

An estimated 148 thousand, or 9%, of the total 1.7 million LEP children were overaged in grade. In contrast, a negligible percentage of the NLEP children was overaged in grade. Nonresponse rate was 14%. The same pattern generally held for both Spanish and non-Spanish language minority groups, although relatively more students in the Spanish language groups were overaged than students in the non-Spanish language minority groups.

Table III-11

Estimated Number of Language Minority Children, Aged 5–14 Years, by Language Background, English Proficiency, and Reading Achievement in the United States: Spring 1978 (Numbers in 000)[a]

Reading Achievement		Total	Proficiency		Spanish	Proficiency		Non-Spanish	Proficiency	
		Total	LEP	NLEP	Total	LEP	NLEP	Total	LEP	NLEP
½ Year or More Above Grade Level	n	777	177	600	281	102	179	496	75	421
	%	25%	10%	44%	17%	9%	35%	35%	14%	49%
At or Close to Grade Level	n	878	433	446	424	285	139	455	148	307
	%	28%	25%	32%	25%	24%	27%	32%	27%	35%
½ to One Year Below Grade level	n	392	282	110	243	185	58	150	97	53
	%	13%	16%	8%	14%	16%	11%	11%	18%	6%
At or Close to One Full Year Below Grade Level	n	243	216	27	170	151	19	72	65	8
	%	8%	13%	2%	10%	13%	4%	5%	12%	1%
More Than One Full Year Below Grade Level	n	424	393	31	311	294	17	113	99	14
	%	14%	23%	2%	19%	25%	3%	8%	18%	2%
No Response	n	383	222	161	253	158	95	130	64	66
	%	12%	13%	12%	15%	13%	19%	9%	12%	8%
Total	n	3,097	1,723	1,375	1,681	1,175	507	1,416	548	868

a. Numbers may not total due to rounding. Regions include California, New York, and the remainder of the country except for Texas.

Table III-12

Estimated Number of Language Minority Children, Aged 5–14 Years, by Language Background, English Proficiency, Grade Retention, and Overagedness in Grade in the United States: Spring 1978 (Numbers in 000)[a]

Variable	Category	n/%	Total — Total	Total — LEP	Total — NLEP	Spanish — Total	Spanish — LEP	Spanish — NLEP	Non-Spanish — Total	Non-Spanish — LEP	Non-Spanish — NLEP
Grade retention	Repeated at Least One Grade or Course	n	214	189	25	154	148	6	59	41	18
		%	7%	11%	2%	9%	13%	1%	4%	7%	2%
	Repeated Part of a Grade	n	37	15	22	37	15	22	b	b	b
		%	1%	1%	2%	2%	1%	4%	0%	0%	0%
	Never Repeated	n	2,151	1,080	1,071	1,187	750	440	964	330	634
		%	69%	63%	78%	71%	64%	86%	68%	60%	73%
	No Record	n	128	116	12	76	73	3	52	43	9
		%	4%	7%	1%	5%	6%	1%	4%	8%	1%
	No Response	n	567	322	245	227	188	39	340	133	206
		%	18%	19%	18%	14%	16%	8%	24%	24%	24%
	Total	n	3,097	1,723	1,375	1,681	1,175	507	1,416	548	868
Overagedness in Grade	Overaged	n	153	148	5	126	125	1	27	23	4
		%	5%	9%	0%	8%	11%	0%	2%	4%	0%
	Not Overaged	n	2,593	1,331	1,261	1,372	909	463	1,220	422	798
		%	84%	77%	92%	82%	77%	91%	86%	77%	92%
	No Response	n	351	244	108	183	141	42	169	103	66
		%	11%	14%	8%	11%	12%	8%	12%	19%	8%
	Total	n	3,097	1,723	1,375	1,681	1,175	507	1,416	548	868

a. Numbers may not total due to rounding. Regions include California, New York, and the remainder of the country except for Texas.

b. Sample size too small to report. Fewer than one thousand.

IV. CONCLUSIONS

The pupil survey of the Children's English and Services Study (CESS) represented the first Federal effort to determine the types of instructional services available nationally to language minority children with limited English proficiency. The study, conducted in Spring 1978, was legislatively mandated in the Bilingual Education Act, as amended, as part of a comprehensive needs assessment for bilingual and other types of educational services. The CESS is one of a number of coordinated studies developed in the U.S. Department of Education to respond to the mandated needs assessment.

A number of conclusions can be drawn from the estimated proportions of children discussed in Chapter III. Some of the conclusions have direct implications for Federal policy, while other conclusions bear upon what has been assumed to be conventional wisdom about bilingual education or language minority children. As will be seen, some of these conventional assumptions are not supported by the results of this study.

First, about one-third of all limited English proficient children appeared to be served by bilingual education, English as a second language instruction, or other special forms of instruction. An estimated 23% of all limited English proficient children received some form of bilingual education, while an additional 11% received ESL independent of those who may have received it as part of their bilingual instruction. Thus, a total of 34% were receiving a special form of educational service beyond standard English-medium instruction.

Second, Federal and State support for special types of instruction appeared to be targeted successfully on children who were in need of the service, independent of the source of support for funding. An estimated 83% of all language minority children receiving support from ESEA Title VII were limited in English proficiency, while 79% of those receiving support from ESEA Title I were limited in English proficiency. Furthermore, approximately 75% of the language minority children receiving support from State bilingual programs were limited in English proficiency. Thus, only

modest percentages of language minority children receiving special forms of targeted instructional support would be considered ineligible based on English language proficiency. Some of these children may be part of a program in compliance with desegregation laws.

Third, the types of bilingual education provided either through Federal or State support do not appear to be focused on maintaining the children's non-English language, and do not appear to draw instructional time away from learning English. Two types of evidence point to these conclusions. The first derives from the percentage of hours in English language instruction received by limited English proficient children in bilingual instruction relative to their limited English proficient peers in English-medium instruction. Whereas approximately 83% of all limited English proficient children in bilingual education received 5 or more hours of instruction in English per week, 76% of the limited English proficient children in English-medium instruction received a comparable number of hours of instruction per week. There was essentially no difference between the percentage of limited English proficient children in bilingual instruction and in English language instruction receiving 10 or more hours of English language instruction per week. The type of English language instruction specified for children in either type of educational approach could have varied, but the overall percentage of children receiving different levels of instruction did not appear to differ. A second type of evidence pointing to these conclusions is the decrease in the percentage of children receiving bilingual instruction from lower to higher grades. There was a sharp drop in the percentage of LEP children receiving bilingual instruction from grades K–13 (54%) to grades 7–9 (17%). This drop suggests that most of the children receiving bilingual instruction do so only for the earlier elementary grades.

Fourth, more limited English proficient children receive support from Federal programs that are *not* specifically designed to provide bilingual instruction than from programs with specific intent to offer bilingual instructional services. An estimated 24% of all limited English proficient children received support from ESEA Title I (Compensatory Education for Disadvantaged Children), while approximately 7% of all limited English proficient children received support from ESEA Title VII (Bilingual Education).

Fifth, assessment of language proficiency was generally restricted to skills in English. While 43% of the limited English proficient children in bilingual instruction were administered tests of English language proficiency, only 24% of the limited English proficient children in bilingual instruction were administered tests of their native language proficiency. These figures indicate that recent proposals to consider native language proficiency or language dominance would require additional assessment over and above that which is normally carried out.

Finally, while the majority of language minority students receiving services are identified as LEP, local education agencies appear to identify fewer limited English proficient children among the total language minority population than are identified by the common English language assessment instrument administered to all children in this study. Schools designated only 24% of the limited English proficient children identified by the test criterion as falling in the range from slightly limited to severely limited in English proficiency. This result probably reflects the differences that exist in identification criteria in general and needs to be considered when interpreting the finding that approximately 34% of LEP students identified by the test were receiving language related services. Quite possibly the remaining students simply were not identified as LEP according to the schools' criteria or may not have been identified initially as language minority. For LEAs, the criteria for identification are apparently less stringent than the ones applied here and point to the need for further research and direction in the area of identification criteria. This conclusion must be stated tentatively, however, because of the high percentage of non-response on this particular questionnaire item (schools did not report information on this item for 42% of the language minority children).

V. REFERENCES

Bruck, M., and Schultz, J. "Language Use in Bilingual Classrooms." Manuscript, undated.

Commissioner's Report on the Condition of Bilingual Education in the Nation. Washington, D.C.: U.S. Office of Education, Department of Health, Education, and Welfare, 1976.

Hartwell, T.; Moore, P.; Weeks, M.; Mason, R.; and Shah, B. *Design Data Collection and Analysis of a Field Test of Instruments and Procedures to Measure English Language Proficiency.* Research Triangle Park, N.C.: Research Triangle Institute, 1976.

Miranda, L., and Associates, Inc. *Children's English and Services Study. Final Report.* Contract No. 400–77–0032. Submitted to the National Institute of Education, February 1979a.

Miranda, L., and Associates, Inc. *Children's English and Services Study. Technical Report on Collection and Analysis of Pupil Survey Responses.* Contract No. 400–77–0032. Submitted to the National Institute of Education, August 1979b.

National Center for Education Statistics. *The Educational Disadvantage of Language Minority Persons in the United States: Spring 1974.* National Center for Education Statistics (NCES) Bulletin 78 B–4. Washington, D.C.: U.S. Department of Health, Education, and Welfare, 1978a.

————. *Geographic Distribution, Nativity, and Age Distribution of Language Minorities in the United States: Spring 1976.* National Center for Education Statistics (NCES) Bulletin 78 B–5. Washington, D.C.: U.S. Department of Health, Education, and Welfare, 1978b.

————. *Place of Birth and Language Characteristics of Persons of Hispanic Origin in the United States: Spring 1976.* National Center for Education Statistics (NCES) Bulletin 78 B–6. Washington, D.C.: U.S. Department of Health, Education, and Welfare, 1978c.

————. *Birthplace and Language Characteristics of Persons of Chinese, Japanese, Korean, Philipino, and Vietnamese Origin in the United States: Spring 1976.* National Center for Education Statistics (NCES) Bulletin 79 B–12. Washington, D.C.: U.S. Department of Health, Education, and Welfare, May 1979.

O'Malley, J. Michael. *Children's English and Services Study: Language Minority Children with Limited English Proficiency in the United States.* Rosslyn, Va.: National Clearinghouse for Bilingual Education, 1981.

Stoltz, W., and Bruck, M. *A Project to Develop a Measure of English Language Proficiency.* Final Report submitted by the Center for Applied Linguistics to the National Center for Education Statistics under Contract No. 300–75–0253. Washington, D.C.: NCES, 1976.

Waggoner, D. "Teacher Resources in Bilingual Education: A National Survey." *Journal of the National Association for Bilingual Education* 3, no. 2 (1979): 53–60.

APPENDIX A

PUPIL SURVEY DESIGN AND DATA COLLECTION

PUPIL SURVEY DESIGN AND DATA COLLECTION

This section of the report on the school survey in the Children's English and Services Study (CESS) provides detail on the conceptual framework for the needs assessment, specifications for the survey questionnaire, the role of the CESS advisory group, pilot tests of the school questionnaire, and response rates for the pupil survey.

Conceptual Framework

The requirements for a survey to count children and for a needs assessment, although stated separately in the legislation, were assumed to be interrelated in planning the CESS. A conceptual framework was required that would allow information on both educational needs and services to be collected in the context of a household survey of language minorities.

The initial framework for the count of limited English proficient children and for the needs assessment was formulated in three questions:

- How many children are in need?

- How many children in need are being served?

- What types of needs do these children have?

The first question, which was concerned with the number of children in need, already was the focus of the effort to count limited English proficient children in the household survey for the CESS. The next two questions were the underlying issues to which the educational needs assessment was addressed. Understanding the number of children who receive different levels of bilingual education would not only provide important information for Congressional deliberations about the scope of future legislation but could also supply information necessary for the Education Department to focus its future program efforts in

bilingual education. The type of educational needs these children demonstrate should also be depicted. The mandate to determine the extent to which educational needs of limited English proficient children are met by Federal, State, and local efforts thus was conceived as a survey of instructional services received by children eligible for bilingual education under ESEA Title VII.

A process for combining the survey of educational needs with the survey of the number of limited English proficient children emerged from this conceptualization of the mandates. In the CESS, parents of language minority children in the household probability sample were requested to permit access to school information. A pupil questionnaire was sent to schools in which these children were enrolled. Schools were asked to indicate the type of instructional services children in the sample received. The questionnaire was sent to schools enrolling non-limited as well as limited English proficient children in the sample. (The distinction between children who were limited versus not limited in English was not made until test data collected on the children were computer scored following the field operations.) Analyses of the school data were designed to reveal full service, partial service, and the absence of service for LEP children.

Definitions were required for *types* and *levels* of service to complete the conceptual framework. The types of bilingual instruction students received could not be determined validly by asking schools to indicate whether children received bilingual programs funded by State or Federal support independently of information about specific program services. Similarly, valid information could not be determined from asking whether children received global program types such as transitional or maintenance bilingual education. As Congress had noted,

Controversies over so-called maintenance or transitional approaches tend to confuse the issue, since these terms mean different things to different people. . . . (House Report on H.R. 15, 1977, p. 87).

Information on types of service could be derived more accurately from identifying components of instruction that States and local education agencies offer to limited English proficient students. Components reported individually or in aggregate patterns could be used to describe program types.

Definition of Instructional Types. The definition for components of instruction was formulated to be compatible with the definition of bilingual education in the Bilingual Education Act of 1974, as amended. No other definition was acceptable because the study originated in mandates in the Act. In ESEA Title VII, a "program of bilingual education" is defined as

. . . a program of instruction designed for children with limited English proficiency in elementary or secondary schools, in which . . .

There is instruction in, and study of, English and, to the extent necessary to allow a child to achieve competence in the English language, the *native language* of the children of limited English proficiency, and such instruction is given with *appreciation for the cultural heritage* of such children, and . . . such instruction shall, to the extent necessary, be in all *courses or subjects* of study which allow a child to progress effectively through the educational system [emphasis added]. Section 703 [a] [4] [A]

The definition of a program of bilingual education in ESEA Title VII contains four components: (1) instruction in English; (2) instruction in the native language of the child; (3) instruction in content areas in the native language; and (4) instruction with appreciation for the cultural background of the child. One or more of these components in varying combinations was used to define instructional types. For example, children in one type of bilingual bicultural instruction receive instruction in English, instruction in language arts of the non-English language, and exposure to culture. In one type of bilingual instruction, the cultural component is absent. An alternative service

type for some children includes only special forms of English language instruction such as English as a second language.

Definition of Instructional Levels. For each instructional type, preliminary indications about the level of service were determined from three **characteristics** of the instruction: (1) the extent to which staff were professional and therefore presumably qualified to offer the component; (2) the number of clock hours in a school week instruction was offered in English and non-English languages; and (3) the extent to which assessment was used for English language proficiency, for reading in the English language and—where appropriate, depending on the instructional type—for reading in the non-English language.

Specifications for the Pupil Survey Questionnaire

The pupil survey questionnaire was developed from content specifications for the instruction components needed to describe a bilingual program, and from the instruction characteristics needed to describe levels of service. The questionnaire derived also from an interest in determining how the school perceived the educational needs of the student, and from an interest in identifying sources of funding for different instructional types.

Portions of the questionnaire concerned with instruction components and characteristics are illustrated in Table A–1, Content Specifications for the Pupil Survey Questionnaire. In the first column are indicated instructional characteristics such as the amount of time instruction was offered, the level of staffing, and assessment approaches used. Across the columns are the instructional components of a bilingual program indicated in ESEA Title VII: English language arts, non-English language arts, cultural studies, and subject areas in the home language. The cell entries show the type of information specified in the questionnaire.

The process by which information indicated in the content specifications was used to depict alternative program types is illustrated in Table A–2, Instructional Typology and Component Services. The first column contains alternative instructional types, and the next column con-

38

Table A–1

Content Specifications for Pupil Survey Questionnaire

Instructional Components

Instructional Characteristics	English Language Arts	Non-English Language Arts	Cultural Studies	Subject Areas in the Non-English Language
Instruction offered to student named (yes or no)	English as a second language, Remedial English language Arts	Only language arts courses	Both English and non-English language instructional areas	Math, Social Studies, and Natural Sciences
Time	Clock hours per week	Clock hours per week	Clock hours per week	Clock hours per week
Staffing (professional or non-professional)	For person who speaks to the child in English	For person who speaks to the child in the non-English language	For person who speaks to the child in either language	For person who speaks to the child in the non-English language
Assessment	Detailed questions about type of assessment in English and in non-English languages and about classification based on these procedures		Not asked	Reading, math, and other in non-English language

tains components appropriate to the respective types. For example, three types of bilingual bicultural instruction are suggested from the component services indicated. Similarly, there are three types of bilingual instruction. Additionally, a variety of non-bilingual instructional types emerge from the classification system, such as the combination of English as a second language with culture. The number of limited English proficient (LEP) and non-limited English Proficient (NLEP) children receiving each instructional type would be indicated in the far right column.

The instructional types represent combinations of component instructional services only. They should *not* be construed to represent a "program" or "model," as might be true of instructional features in an integrated series of objectives, instructional patterns, and assessment procedures. The degree to which instructional features were integrated is suggested by indices of the level at which the instruction is offered. For each instructional type, the level at which the service is provided was determined from the staffing pattern, the number of clock hours, and the type of assessment provided.

Table A–2

Instructional Typology and Component Services

Type of Instruction	Components[a]	Proficiency[b]		
		Total	LEP	NLEP
Bilingual Bicultural: A	ELI, CULT, NELA, CONT			
Bilingual Bicultural: B	ELI, CULT, NELA			
Bilingual Bicultural: C	ELI, CULT, CONT			
Bilingual: A	ELI, NELA, CONT			
Bilingual: B	ELI, NELA			
Bilingual: C	ELI, CONT			
ELI	ELI, CULT			
	ELI Only			
ESL	ESL, CULT			
	ESL Only			
Other				

a. ELI: English language instruction, composed of English as a second language (ESL), English language arts, or remedial or corrective instruction in English

NELA: Non-English language arts

CONT: Content area instruction through the non-English language in math, social studies, natural science, or other areas.

CULT: Culture offered either in English or the non-English language

b. LEP: Limited English proficient

NLEP: Non-limited English Proficient

Role of the CESS Advisory Group

The advisory group performed the following functions in development of the needs assessment: (1) review the conceptual design; (2) develop questionnaire items corresponding to the content specifications; and (3) delineate characteristics for levels of the different program types.

Conceptual Design. Advisory group comments were obtained at two stages in the conceptual design. At the first stage, the conceptual framework discussed above had yet to be developed. The advisory group was requested to recommend an initial conceptual design for the needs assessment. One option considered early for reflecting needs of limited English proficient children was to report only test score data in achievement areas and other performance indices, regardless of instructional services received. In commenting on this option, the advisory group noted that in their view the educational needs of limited English proficient students were not substantially different from the educational needs of other children apart from the language area. Further, they maintained that although test scores might reflect student needs to a degree, test scores failed to reflect efforts by schools to address the needs. Consequently, to base the needs assessment on test data irrespective of educational services seemed ill advised. Collecting information on educational services was considered essential to the needs assessment.

At the second stage, the advisory group was requested to comment on a preliminary version of the conceptual design discussed above that portrayed types and levels of instruction. Following discussion in the large group, a working group refined the design and defined alternative program types and ways of obtaining information about level of services.

Questionnaire Items. Final items on the pupil survey questionnaire (Appendix B) were developed by a task force of the advisory group. The task force reviewed the contribution of each item on the questionnaire to the overall purposes of the study and to the legislative mandates. The item format underwent revision following pilot tests of the pupil survey questionnaire, but in principle the substance was retained.

Program Types and Levels of Service. The pupil survey questionnaire was designed to yield information about instructional services received by limited English proficient students. Although content specifications for the items and item substance had been developed and pilot tested, a detailed approach for aggregating item-level results to produce the level and types of service remained to be determined. For this purpose, a second task force reviewed the questionnaire items and formulated an analysis plan for identifying whether students received particular types of instruction, and for determining the level at which the instructional types were received. The task force comprised State Directors of Bilingual Education or their designates in four States with heavy concentrations of language minorities, and staff from the U.S. Office of Bilingual Education, the National Institute of Education, and the National Center for Education Statistics.

The task force identified item responses on the pupil survey questionnaire that suggested that a student received specific instructional components. Receipt of a particular instructional type could be determined from unique combinations of components. For example, in one type of bilingual bicultural instruction, the school offered instruction in the following components: (1) English through any combination of English as a second language (ESL), English langue arts, or remedial or corrective instruction in English; (2) language arts of the child's non-English language or content areas through the student's non-English language; and (3) culture associated with the language background of the child. Although ESL is often cited in the literature as a necessary component of bilingual instruction, the task force noted that the ESEA Title VII legislative definition of a "program of bilingual education" stipulated instruction in English generally rather than instruction in ESL specifically.

The task force also provided criteria for the level of instructional types, using three characteristics: (1) staff requirements, (2) clock hours of instruction, and (3) type of assessment. The task force determined that all instructional staff should be professional without exception, regardless of the component or instructional type. Time requirements for components differed, depending on the instructional type. For bilingual or bilingual bicultural instruction, the task force required 5 hours in English and 5 hours in the non-English language. Assessment in this type of instruction must be administered to the student in English for language proficiency and in the non–English language for oral/listening skills plus reading. The requirements for other instructional types differed, as shown in Table A–3, Component Requirements for Instructional Typology.

In preparing specifications for level within type, the task force recognized the limitations of a mailout, self-report questionnaire. The self-report questionnaire, even with an extensive pilot test, should in this study be considered to provide only tentative information in the absence of on-site verification.

Further, using school self-report of instructional services is likely to provide the upward boundary if not an overestimate of the number of children served. Schools may prefer to depict services in a favorable manner. Further, reports that services are provided reveal nothing about the quality of the services even when information is obtained on the level of the services.

Field Data Collection

Data collection for the pupil survey questionnaire occurred in two phases. Phase I coincided with the CESS household data collection

Table A–3

Component Requirements for Instructional Typology[a]

Instructional Type	ELI	NELI	STAFF	ASSESS
Bilingual Bicultural (subtypes A,B,C)	5 clock hours/ week in any combination of ESL, ELA, or Remedial Corrective Instruction in English (RCE)	5 clock hours/ week in any combination of NELA, CONT, and CULT	Professional in all areas	Use English language standardized test
	CULT required, depending on subtype, with NELA, CONT, or CULT		Same	Use non-English language standardized test of language and reading
Bilingual (Subtypes A,B,C)	5 clock hours/ week in any combination of ESL, ELA, or RCE	5 clock hours/ week in any combination of NELA and CONT –and– Either NELA or CONT required	Same	Same
ESL/CULT	5 clock hours/ week in ESL, CULT required	None required	Same	Use English language standardized test.

a. ELI: English language instruction, composed of English as a second language (ESL), English language arts (ELA), or remedial or corrective instruction in English (RCE),
   NELI: Non-English language institution
   NELA: Non-English language arts
   CONT: Content area instruction through the non-English language in math, social studies, natural science, or other area
   CULT: Culture offered either in English or the non-English language
   ASSESS: Assessment in English and, where appropriate, in the non-English language

effort in Spring 1978. Phase II was a special follow-up in Spring 1979 designed to increase the response rate.

Procedures followed in each phase were essentially identical, with two exceptions. First, items on the pupil survey questionnaire in the follow-up phase were reworded for retrospective data collection to Spring 1978. Second, students in the 15- through 18-year-old range were not sampled in the follow-up because of funding limitations. The second phase was undertaken only after a detailed examination of procedures and results from the first phase revealed that (1) responses in Spring 1978 were provided by responsible school authorities; (2) retrospective data to Spring 1978 would be available; and (3) State-level cooperation would be available in key States necessary to increase the response rate. This report presents results only for the 5–14 year olds for both phases combined.

Pupil questionnaires were mailed to schools enrolling eligible students aged 5–14 years. Eligible students were defined as those with valid English language test results and signed parental consent forms releasing school information. Clearances for access to schools were obtained according to Federal requirements following procedures prescribed by State and local education agencies or by private schools, wherever students were enrolled. Questionnaires and parent consent forms were mailed to a coordinator for the study who was located, depending on State procedures, in the school, the local education agency, or the State education agency. The coordinator was the contact for call-backs to assure that questionnaires were received and to obtain information needed to complete questionnaires that were received with partial answers. Up to four telephone call-backs were made to each coordinator.

Response Rates

Response rates to the school survey for language minority children in the CESS are shown in Table A–4, Response Rates by Subpopulation for the Parent Consent Form and the Pupil Survey Questionnaire. Response rates for the parent consent form were 95% or more in each subpopulation, indicating that parents of nearly all language minority children in the sample

were willing to approve the release of school information on their children for the purposes of the study. The response rate for the pupil survey questionnaire among schools enrolling sample language minority children in New York was 64%. In California and Texas, the pupil survey questionnaire response rates were far too low to permit reporting the results by State despite strong follow-up and support for the study at the State level. The response rate in the remainder of the country, 79%, was relatively high and indicates acceptable cooperation for making estimates of educational needs and school services. The differential pattern of response rates by subpopulation does not enable subpopulation level analyses to be performed as was originally anticipated. Further, even in regions with an acceptable response rate, the numbers do not permit detailed analyses because cell sizes would be too small. Therefore, data for California, New York, and the remainder of the country were combined in the analysis. The response rate in these areas for the parent consent form was 97% and for the pupil survey questionnaire was 67%.

The response rates by subpopulation in part reflect local education agency cooperation; they also reflect the type of clearance procedures that States require of contractors for the Federal Government. A description of Texas and California State Education Agency procedures for permitting the Federal contractor to gain access to local education agencies enrolling students in the study will serve to illustrate differences in the clearance procedures.

The process by which local school cooperation was requested in Texas resulted in a particularly low response rate, even though the Texas Chief State School Officer had supported the study in correspondence to local superintendents of instruction whose districts enrolled students identified in the CESS sample. An enclosed post card, self-addressed to the State Education Agency, enabled the superintendents to indicate whether or not they wished to participate in the study. Of 21 school districts in Texas, 6 refused, 5 agreed to participate, and 10 failed to return the post card even after a follow-up letter. Contacts by the Federal contractor were permitted only to districts that agreed to cooperate. In contrast, in California

Table A–4

Detailed Information on Response Rates by Subpopulation for the Parent Consent Form and Pupil Survey Questionnaire[a]

Component	Subpopulation	Eligible	Completed		Not Completed	
		n	n	p	n	p
Parent Consent	California	310	301	.97	9	.03
Form	Texas	460	436	.95	24	.05
	New York	279	274	.98	5	.02
	Remainder	860	828	.96	32	.04
	Total	1909	1839	.96	70	.04
Pupil Survey	California	301	114	.38	187	.62
Questionnaire[b]	Texas	436	43	.10	393	.90
	New York	274	175	.64	99	.36
	Remainder	828	655	.79	173	.21
	Total	1839	987	.54	852	.46

a. Includes 5– to 14-year-old children only.
b. Figures in the Eligible column exclude students who were not enrolled in school.

the Federal contractor was permitted to contact the local district, and the State Office of Bilingual Education was permitted by the Chief State School Officer to contact school districts directly in support of the study. It seems possible that future studies in California would produce larger response rates through sending interviewers to the schools. In Texas, this approach would not be possible unless the State clearance procedures were modified. NIE had requested a modification of the State clearance procedures in the Texas follow-up, but the request was not approved by SEA.

Nonresponse adjustments for the parent consent form and the pupil questionnaire for each region were determined from the inverse of the ratio of completed questionnaires to total eligible students. This nonresponse adjustment was appended to the CESS basic weighting procedures. Analyses to inspect the comparability between students in nonresponding versus responding schools were not possible for the purposes of this report. However, comparisons by subpopulation of the weighted

number of limited English proficient (LEP) and non-limited English proficient (NLEP) children in the household survey and the school survey reveal that the numbers of LEP and NLEP children in the school survey were underestimated in some subpopulations and overestimated in others. This analysis is presented in Table A–5, Comparison of Household and School Surveys by Subpopulation for Limited English Proficient (LEP) and Non-limited English Proficient (NLEP) Children.

The most noticeable example of lack of comparability is in California, where the response rate was only 38%. The estimated number of LEP children in California was 594 thousand from the household survey but only 417 thousand from the school survey. In New York, where the response rate was 64%, the estimated number of LEP children was 458 thousand in the household survey and 471 thousand in the school survey. In the remainder of the country, the estimated number of LEP children was 908 thousand in the household survey and 834 thousand in the school survey. For California,

Table A–5

Comparison of Household and School Surveys
by Subpopulations for Estimated Number of Limited English Proficient (LEP)
and Non-limited English Proficient (NLEP) Children
(Numbers in 000)

Subpopulation	Total		LEP		NLEP	
	House-hold	School	House-hold	School	House hold	School
California	855	834	594	417	261	417
Texas	a	b	a	b	a	b
New York	608	592	458	471	150	121
Remainder	1,718	1,671	908	834	810	837
Total	3,181	3,097	1,960	1,723	1,221	1,375

a. Numbers omitted to make column totals comparable
b. Response rate too small to report.

New York, and the remainder of the country combined, excepting Texas, the LEP estimate was 1.96 million in the household survey and 1.7 million in the school survey.

The lack of comparability between the home and the school surveys results from differences in the basic sample weights for two groups of children: those on whom school information was received, and those on whom school information was not received. The nonresponse adjustment for the school survey is employed in the assumption that there are no systematic differences between the basic sampling weights of the two groups. In the absence of differences, the nonresponse adjustment corrects for the missing cases, and estimates derived from the household and school surveys will be equal. However, if the basic sample weights are larger for children with school information than for children with no school information, the estimated numbers of children in the school survey will be larger to a corresponding degree.

The pattern of differences between home and school surveys for estimated numbers of LEP and NLEP children in some cases produced larger estimates for the home survey and in other cases larger estimates for the school survey, depending on the subpopulation and the language classification of the children. In the aggregate across states, however, the estimate of LEP children differed by 12% and the estimate of NLEP children differed by 11%.

Comparisons were made between the household and school survey-weighted numbers for LEP and NLEP children by language (Spanish, other) aggregated across California, New York, and the remainder of the country, excepting Texas. In no case was the difference between household and school surveys for LEP or NLEP children of a particular language background greater than 11%, and the differences generally were smaller. Comparable analyses were performed by age with similar results.

The possible impact of differences discussed above between the results of the home and school surveys cannot be identified in the absence of additional data analyses.

APPENDIX B

PUPIL SURVEY QUESTIONNAIRE

CHILDREN'S ENGLISH & SERVICES STUDY

CONDUCTED FOR:

National Institute of Education
National Center for Education Statistics
and
U.S. Office of Education

CONDUCTED BY:

L. Miranda & Associates, Inc.
with
Westat, Inc.
and
Resource Development Institute

PUPIL SURVEY QUESTIONNAIRE

Assurances

ENTER THE NAME(S) AND AGE(S) OF THE TARGET CHILD(REN) FROM THE HOUSEHOLD
ENUMERATION ON PAGE 3 OF THE SCREENER.

BOX A

ASK H-1 THROUGH H-32 FOR ONE TARGET CHILD BEFORE PROCEEDING WITH THE OTHER TARGET
CHILD(REN), IF ANY. IF THE TARGET CHILDREN HAVE DIFFERENT PARENTS OR GUARDIANS,
ASK ALL QUESTIONS APPROPRIATE FOR ONE PARENT BEFORE ASKING TO SPEAK TO THE SECOND
PARENT.

H-1.   Is *(TARGET CHILD)* enrolled or attending school now?

                         Yes ....

                         No ....

H-2.   Please tell me the name and address of the school *(TARGET CHILD)* is
         enrolled in. (CHILD MAY ATTEND TWO SCHOOLS. ALSO TRY TO OBTAIN THE
         NAME OF THE SCHOOL DISTRICT.)

H-3.   Is *(SCHOOL)* a public or private school?

                                   FIRST SCHOOL:

                                       Public ....

                                       Private ....

                                   SECOND SCHOOL:

                                       Public ....

                                       Private ....

50

BOX A			
	/////////	/////////	/////////
H-1.	......1(H-2) ......2(H-5)	......1(H-2) ......2(H-5)	......1(H-2) ......2(H-5)
H-2.	FIRST SCHOOL: Name:_____ Address:_____ _____ _____ Zip:_____ District:_____ SECOND SCHOOL: Name:_____ Address:_____ _____ _____ Zip:_____ District:_____	FIRST SCHOOL: Name:_____ Address:_____ _____ _____ Zip:_____ District:_____ SECOND SCHOOL: _____ _____ _____ _____ Zip:_____ District:_____	FIRST SCHOOL: Name:_____ Address:_____ _____ _____ Zip:_____ District:_____ SECOND SCHOOL: _____ _____ _____ _____ Zip:_____ District:_____
H-3.	...... 1 ...... 2 ...... 1 2	...... 1 ...... 2 ...... 1 2	...... 1 ...... 2 ...... 1 2

H-4.   Is *(TARGET CHILD)* the same name in which he/she appears in the school records or is he/she listed under a different name?

The same name ....

A different name (SPECIFY):........

H-5.   Why isn't *(TARGET CHILD)* enrolled in school now?   (READ ALL CATEGORIES AND CIRCLE AS MANY AS APPLY.)

HAND
CARD 1

Is too young ....

Is too ill or handicapped ....

Dropped out ....

Suspended or expelled ....

Needed at home ....

Went to work ....

Family moved ....

Other (SPECIFY): ....

H-6.   Was there something about school that led *(TARGET CHILD)* to leave school?   (READ ALL CATEGORIES AND CIRCLE AS MANY AS APPLY.)

HAND
CARD 2

Disliked school ....

Couldn't understand instruction in English ....

Found school work too difficult ....

Had to repeat too many grades ....

Other (SPECIFY): ....

No ....

H-7.   What is the highest grade or year of regular school *(TARGET CHILD)* has ever attended? (ENTER CODE IN COLUMN.)

20 = Never attended   04 = Fourth grade   10 = Tenth grade

21 = Prekindergarten   05 = Fifth grade   11 = Eleventh grade

22 = Kindergarten   06 = Sixth grade   12 = Twelfth grade

01 = First grade   07 = Seventh grade   13 = First year college

02 = Second grade   08 = Eighth grade   14 = Second year college

03 = Third grade   09 = Ninth grade   15 = Other (SPECIFY)

H-8.   Did *(TARGET CHILD)* complete that grade (year)?

Yes ....

No ....

52

H-4.	... 1 ... 2 _____ } (H-7)	... 1 ... 2 _____ } (H-7)	... 1 ... 2 _____ } (H-7)
H-5.	... 1 (H-7) ... 2 (H-7) ... 3 (H-6) ... 4 (H-7) ... 5 (H-7) ... 6 (H-7) ... 7 (H-7) ... 8 _____ (H-7)	... 1 (H-7) ... 2 (H-7) ... 3 (H-6) ... 4 (H-7) ... 5 (H-7) ... 6 (H-7) ... 7 (H-7) ... 8 _____ (H-7)	... 1 (H-7) ... 2 (H-7) ... 3 (H-6) ... 4 (H-7) ... 5 (H-7) ... 6 (H-7) ... 7 (H-7) ... 8 _____ (H-7)
H-6.	... 1 ... 2 ... 3 ... 4 ... 5_____ _____ ... 6	... 1 ... 2 ... 3 ... 4 ... 5_____ _____ ... 6	... 1 ... 2 ... 3 ... 4 ... 5_____ _____ ... 6
H-7.	_____ Number	_____ Number	_____ Number
H-8.	... 1 ... 2 } (Box B)	... 1 ... 2 } (Box B)	... 1 ... 2 } (Box B)

```
┌─────────┐
│  BOX B  │
└─────────┘
```

ASK H-9 THROUGH H-12 ONLY IF *(TARGET CHILD)* WAS BORN OUTSIDE THE U.S. (REFER
TO S-19). OTHERWISE, SKIP TO H-13. BE SURE TO CHECK IN BOX B.

H-9.   Did *(TARGET CHILD)* attend school before coming to the U.S.?

                                    Yes ....

                                    No ....

H-10.   For how many years did *(TARGET CHILD)* attend school before coming
          to the U.S.?   (ENTER CODE IN COLUMN.)

     00 = Less than one year   06 = Six years   12 = Twelve years
     01 = One year   07 = Seven years   13 = Thirteen years
     02 = Two years   08 = Eight years   14 = Fourteen years
     03 = Three years   09 = Nine years   15 = Other (SPECIFY)
     04 = Four years   10 = Ten years
     05 = Five years   11 = Eleven years

H-11.   In what language was *(TARGET CHILD)* taught subjects such as
          arithmetic, science, and history?

                                    English ....

                                    Language other than English ......

H-12.   For how many years?
                                    One year ....

                                    Two years ....

                                    Three years ....

                                    Four years ....

                                    Five or more years ....

H-13.   Can *(TARGET CHILD)* speak English?

                                    Yes ....

                                    No ....

H-14.   How well does *(TARGET CHILD)* speak English? Very well, well, not well?

                                    Very well ....

                                    Well (all right) ....
                                                     ⎧ (More than a few words)
                       PROBE ──────▶ Not well ⎨
                                                     ⎩ (Just a few words).....
                                    Not at all ....

54
```
```

BOX B	☐ Born in U.S. (H-13) ☐ Born outside U.S.	☐ Born in U.S. (H-13) ☐ Born outside U.S.	☐ Born in U.S.(H-13) ☐ Born outside U.S.
H-9.	... 1 (H-10) ... 2 (H-13)	... 1 (H-10) ... 2 (H-13)	... 1 (H-10) ... 2 (H-13)
H-10.	_____ Number	_____ Number	_____ Number
H-11.	... 1 (H-12) ... 2 (H-13)	... 1 (H-12) ... 2 (H-13)	... 1 (H-12) ... 2 (H-13)
H-12.	... 1 ... 2 ... 3 ... 4 ... 5	... 1 ... 2 ... 3 ... 4 ... 5	... 1 ... 2 ... 3 ... 4 ... 5
H-13.	... 1 (H-14) ... 2 (H-15)	... 1 (H-14) ... 2 (H-15)	... 1 (H-14) ... 2 (H-15)
H-14.	... 1 ... 2 ... 3 ... 4 ... 5	... 1 ... 2 ... 3 ... 4 ... 5	... 1 ... 2 ... 3 ... 4 ... 5

H-15.   Can (TARGET CHILD) understand spoken English?

                              Yes ....

                              No ....

H-16.   How well does (TARGET CHILD) understand spoken English? Very well,
        well, not well?

                              Very well ....

                              Well (all right) ....
                                              ⎧ (More than a few words)
                      PROBE ──▶Not well ⎨
                                              ⎩ (Just a few words).....
                              Not at all ....

H-17.   Can (TARGET CHILD) read and write English?

                              Yes ....

                              No ....

H-18.   How well does (TARGET CHILD) read and write English? Very well,
        well, not well?

                              Very well ....

                              Well (all right) ....
                                              ⎧ (More than a few words)
                      PROBE ──▶Not well ⎨
                                              ⎩ (Just a few words).....
                              Not at all ....

H-15.	... 1 (H-16) ... 2 (H-17)	... 1 (H-16) ... 2 (H-17)	... 1 (H-16) ... 2 (H-17)
H-16.	... 1 ... 2 ... 3 ... 4 ... 5	... 1 ... 2 ... 3 ... 4 ... 5	... 1 ... 2 ... 3 ... 4 ... 5
H-17.	... 1 (H-18) ... 2 (Box C)	... 1 (H-18) ... 2 (Box C)	... 1 (H-18) ... 2 (Box C)
H-18.	... 1 ... 2 ... 3 } (Box C) ... 4 ... 5	... 1 ... 2 ... 3 } (Box C) ... 4 ... 5	... 1 ... 2 ... 3 } (Box C) ... 4 ... 5

BOX C

IN H-19 THROUGH H-22, NON-ENGLISH HOME LANGUAGE REFERS TO THE NON-ENGLISH LANGUAGE THAT IS USUALLY OR OFTEN SPOKEN BY THE PEOPLE IN THE HOUSEHOLD (REFER TO S-2 AND S-3 ON THE SCREENER). IF THE RESPONSES TO BOTH S-2 AND S-3 ARE NON-ENGLISH LANGUAGES, ASK ABOUT S-2, THE LANGUAGE USUALLY SPOKEN. BE SURE TO ENTER THIS LANGUAGE IN BOX C.

H-19. Can *(TARGET CHILD)* speak and understand spoken *(NON-ENGLISH HOME LANGUAGE)*?

Yes ....

No ....

H-20. How well does *(TARGET CHILD)* speak and understand spoken *(NON-ENGLISH HOME LANGUAGE)*? Very well, well, not well?

Very well ....

Well (all right) ....
(More than a few words)
PROBE ⟶ Not well {
(Just a few words).....
Not at all......................

H-21. Can *(TARGET CHILD)* read and write *(NON-ENGLISH HOME LANGUAGE)*?

Yes ....

No ....

H-22. How well does *(TARGET CHILD)* read and write *(NON-ENGLISH HOME LANGUAGE)*? Very well, well, not well?

Very well ....

Well (all right) ....
(More than a few words)
PROBE ⟶ Not well {
(Just a few words).....
Not at all ....

58

BOX C	NON-ENGLISH HOME LANGUAGE		
H-19.	... 1 *(H-20)* ... 2 *(H-21)*	... 1 *(H-20)* ... 2 *(H-21)*	... 1 *(H-20)* ... 2 *(H-21)*
H-20.	... 1 ... 2 ... 3 ... 4 ... 5	... 1 ... 2 ... 3 ... 4 ... 5	... 1 ... 2 ... 3 ... 4 ... 5
H-21.	... 1 *(H-22)* ... 2 *(Box D)*	... 1 *(H-22)* ... 2 *(Box D)*	... 1 *(H-22)* ... 2 *(Box D)*
H-22.	... 1 ... 2 ... 3 } *(Box D)* ... 4 ... 5	... 1 ... 2 ... 3 } *(Box D)* ... 4 ... 5	... 1 ... 2 ... 3 } *(Box D)* ... 4 ... 5

```
┌─────────────────────────────────────────────────────────────────────────┐
│                            ┌──────────┐                                   │
│                            │  BOX  D  │                                   │
│                            └──────────┘                                   │
│                                                                           │
│  ASK H-23 ONLY IF (TARGET CHILD) HAS BROTHERS OR SISTERS (REFER TO S-11). │
│  OTHERWISE, SKIP TO H-24.  BE SURE TO CHECK IN BOX D.                      │
│                                                                           │
├───────────────────────────────────────────────────────────────────────────┤
│                                                                           │
│  H-23.      What language does (TARGET CHILD) usually speak to his/her brothers │
│             and sisters?   (ENTER CODE IN COLUMN.)                        │
│  ┌──────┐   01 = English               11 = Navajo                        │
│  │ HAND │                                                                 │
│  │CARD 3│   02 = Arabic                12 = Polish                         │
│  └──────┘                                                                 │
│             03 = Chinese               13 = Portuguese                    │
│                                                                           │
│             04 = Filipino (Tagalog, Ilocano)  14 = Russian                │
│                                                                           │
│             05 = French                15 = Scandinavian language         │
│                                                                           │
│             06 = German                16 = Spanish                       │
│                                                                           │
│             07 = Greek                 17 = Vietnamese                     │
│                                                                           │
│             08 = Italian               18 = Yiddish                       │
│                                                                           │
│             09 = Japanese              19 = Other (SPECIFY)                │
│                                                                           │
│             10 = Korean                                                   │
│                                                                           │
├───────────────────────────────────────────────────────────────────────────┤
│                                                                           │
│  H-24       What language does (TARGET CHILD) usually speak to his/her best │
│             friends?   (ENTER CODE IN COLUMN.)                            │
│  ┌──────┐   01 = English               11 = Navajo                        │
│  │ HAND │                                                                 │
│  │CARD 3│   02 = Arabic                12 = Polish                         │
│  └──────┘                                                                 │
│             03 = Chinese               13 = Portuguese                    │
│                                                                           │
│             04 = Filipino (Tagalog, Ilocano)  14 = Russian                │
│                                                                           │
│             05 = French                15 = Scandinavian language         │
│                                                                           │
│             06 = German                16 = Spanish                       │
│                                                                           │
│             07 = Greek                 17 = Vietnamese                     │
│                                                                           │
│             08 = Italian               18 = Yiddish                       │
│                                                                           │
│             09 = Japanese              19 = Other (SPECIFY)                │
│                                                                           │
│             10 = Korean                20 = Don't know                     │
│                                                                           │
└───────────────────────────────────────────────────────────────────────────┘
```

60

BOX D	☐ Has brothers or sisters	☐ Has brothers or sisters	☐ Has brothers or sisters
	☐ Does <u>not</u> have brothers or sisters *(H-24)*	☐ Does <u>not</u> have brothers or sisters *(H-24)*	☐ Does <u>not</u> have brothers or sisters *(H-24)*
H-23.	_____ Number	_____ Number	_____ Number
H-24.	_____ *(Box E)* Number	_____ *(Box E)* Number	_____ *(Box E)* Number

BEFORE ASKING H-25 THROUGH H-32, REFER TO H-1.

- IF *(TARGET CHILD)* IS CURRENTLY ENROLLED IN OR ATTENDING SCHOOL, SAY:

  As I told you, we will be going to *(TARGET CHILD'S)* school to find out what he/she is being taught in school, but now I would like to know if *(TARGET CHILD)* is receiving any instruction in <u>English</u> from anywhere besides a regular school?

  Yes ....

  No ....

- IF *(TARGET CHILD)* IS NOT CURRENTLY ENROLLED IN OR ATTENDING SCHOOL, SAY:

  Now I would like to know if *(TARGET CHILD)* is receiving any instruction in <u>English</u> from anywhere besides a regular school?

  Yes ....

  No ....

H-25.   What is *(TARGET CHILD)* being taught to do in English?   (READ EACH CATEGORY AND CIRCLE YES OR NO FOR EACH.)

| HAND CARD 4 |

To speak the language better ....

To understand the spoken language better ....

To read the language better ....

To write the language better ....

Mathematics ....

Science ....

Social Studies ....

Other (SPECIFY): ....

H-26   Who is teaching it?   (READ ALL CATEGORIES AND CIRCLE AS MANY AS APPLY.)

| HAND CARD 5 |

Mother, father, sister, or brother of *(TARGET CHILD)*.......

Another relative or a friend or acquaintance ....

Teacher ....

Private, paid tutor ....

Other (SPECIFY) ....

BOX E	☐ Enrolled in school
	
	   ... 1(*H-25*)
	
	   ... 2(*H-28*)
	
	☐ <u>Not</u> enrolled
	   <u>in</u> school
	
	   ... 1(*H-25*)
	
	   ... 2(*H-28*)
		☐ Enrolled in school
		
		   ... 1(*H-25*)
		
		   ... 2(*H-28*)
		
		☐ <u>Not</u> enrolled
		   <u>in</u> school
		
		   ... 1(*H-25*)
		
		   ... 2(*H-28*)
			☐ Enrolled in school
			
			   ... 1(*H-25*)
			
			   ... 2(*H-28*)
			
			☐ <u>Not</u> enrolled
			   <u>in</u> school
			
			   ... 1(*H-25*)
			
			   ... 2(*H-28*)

H-25	<u>Yes</u> <u>No</u> 1 2 1 2 1 2 1 2 1 2 1 2 1 2 _____	<u>Yes</u> <u>No</u> 1 2 1 2 1 2 1 2 1 2 1 2 1 2 _____	<u>Yes</u> <u>No</u> 1 2 1 2 1 2 1 2 1 2 1 2 1 2 _____

H-26.	... 1 ... 2 ... 3 ... 4 ... 5 _____ _____	... 1 ... 2 ... 3 ... 4 ... 5 _____ _____	... 1 ... 2 ... 3 ... 4 ... 5 _____ _____

H-27.   Where is it being taught? (READ ALL CATEGORIES AND CIRCLE AS MANY AS
         APPLY.)

                    In a church building ....

         ┌────────┐ In a community organization or social service agency
         │ HAND │ (YMCA, etc.) ....
         │ CARD │
         │   6   │ In a school building ....
         └────────┘
                    In the home of (TARGET CHILD), a friend, relative or tutor.

                    Other (SPECIFY)..

H-28.   Is (TARGET CHILD) receiving any instruction in any language other
         than English from anywhere besides a regular school?

                              Yes ....

                              No ....

H-29.   In what language?   (ENTER CODE IN COLUMN.)

                    02 = Arabic   11 = Navajo

         ┌────────┐ 03 = Chinese   12 = Polish
         │ HAND │
         │ CARD 3 │ 04 = Filipino (Tagalog, Ilocano) 13 = Portuguese
         └────────┘
                    05 = French   14 = Russian

                    06 = German   15 = Scandinavian language

                    07 = Greek   16 = Spanish

                    08 = Italian   17 = Vietnamese

                    09 = Japanese   18 = Yiddish

                    10 = Korean   19 = Other (SPECIFY)

H-27.	... 1 ... 2 ... 3 ... 4 ... 5 _____ _____	... 1 ... 2 ... 3 ... 4 ... 5 _____ _____	... 1 ... 2 ... 3 ... 4 ... 5 _____ _____
H-28.	... 1 *(H-29)* ... 2 *(Box F)*	... 1 *(H-29)* ... 2 *(Box F)*	... 1 *(H-29)* ... 2 *(Box F)*
H-29.	_____ Number	_____ Number	_____ Number

H-30.   What is *(TARGET CHILD)* being taught to do in *(LANGUAGE)*? (**READ EACH** CATEGORY AND CIRCLE YES OR NO FOR EACH.)

	To speak the language better ....
HAND CARD 4	To understand the spoken language better ....
	To read the language better ....
	To write the language better ....
	Mathematics ....
	Science ....
	Social Studies ....
	Other (SPECIFY): ....

H-31.   Who is teaching it? (**READ ALL CATEGORIES AND CIRCLE AS MANY AS APPLY.**)

	Mother, father, sister, or brother of *(TARGET CHILD)* ....
HAND CARD 5	Another relative or a friend or acquaintance ....
	Teacher ....
	Private, paid tutor ....
	Other (SPECIFY):...................................

H-32.   Where is it being taught? (**READ ALL CATEGORIES AND CIRCLE AS MANY AS** APPLY.)

	In a church building ....
HAND CARD 6	In a community organization or social service agency (YMCA, etc.) ....
	In a school building ....
	In the home of *(TARGET CHILD)*, a friend, relative, or tutor ....
	Other (SPECIFY):...................................

BOX F

IF MORE THAN ONE TARGET CHILD, GO BACK TO H-1 ON PAGE 1.   OTHERWISE, GO TO H-33.

	TARGET CHILD 1	TARGET CHILD 2	TARGET CHILD 3
	Last name:	Last name:	Last name:
	First name:	First name:	First name:
	Age:_____	Age:_____	Age:_____

	Yes	No	Yes	No	Yes	No
	1	2	1	2	1	2
	1	2	1	2	1	2
	1	2	1	2	1	2
H-30.	1	2	1	2	1	2
	1	2	1	2	1	2
	1	2	1	2	1	2
	1	2	1	2	1	2
	1	2	1	2	1	2
	_____		_____		_____	

	TARGET CHILD 1	TARGET CHILD 2	TARGET CHILD 3
	... 1	... 1	... 1
	... 2	... 2	... 2
H-31.	... 3	... 3	... 3
	... 4	... 4	... 4
	... 5 _____	... 5 _____	... 5 _____
	_____	_____	_____
	_____	_____	_____

	TARGET CHILD 1	TARGET CHILD 2	TARGET CHILD 3
	... 1	... 1	... 1
	... 2	... 2	... 2
H-32.	... 3 } Box F	... 3 } Box F	... 3 } Box F
	... 4	... 4	... 4
	... 5 _____	... 5 _____	... 5 _____
	_____	_____	_____

H-33.   Last year (1977), did any member of your family (14 years or older)
         living here work, even for a few days?

                                    Yes 1

                                    No .... 2 *(H-35)*

H-34.   How many members of your family worked last year?

                                    _____
                                              Number

H-35.   Last year (1977), did any member of your family receive any earnings
         or income from any of the following sources? All may not apply to
         you or your family, but it is easiest if I ask you about each one at
         a time.   (READ EACH CATEGORY AND CIRCLE YES, NO, DON'T KNOW FOR
         EACH.)

                              ┌──────────┐
                              │ HAND   │
                              │ CARD 7 │
                              └──────────┘

Source of Income	Yes	No	Don't Know
1. Wages or salaries	1	2	8
2. Own farm or nonfarm business, partnership, or professional practice	1	2	8
3. Dividends, interest, property rental	1	2	8
4. Unemployment or Workmen's Compensation ...	1	2	8
5. Social Security or retirement	1	2	8
6. Welfare payments for aid to dependent children	1	2	8
7. Any (other) public assistance or welfare payments (include old age assistance, aid to the blind or totally disabled, general assistance)	1	2	8
8. Alimony or child support	1	2	8
9. Regular contributions from persons not in this family or anything else	1	2	8

H-36.   What was the total combined income of all members of this family in
         1977? Include income from all sources such as wages, salaries, Social
         Security or retirement benefits, help from relatives, rent from
         property, and so forth. Please read me the letter only.

                                    _____
                                              Letter
      ┌──────────┐
      │ HAND   │   Refused 97
      │ CARD 8 │
      └──────────┘   Don't know 98

         ENTER THE PERSON NUMBER (FROM PAGE 3 OF THE SCREENER) OF THE RESPONDENT
         FOR H-33 THROUGH H-36. _____

                                        68

H-37.   Since we're interested in how children's use of English changes as they get older, at some time in the future, we will need to talk again with some of the persons we are interviewing now. We don't know who these persons will be as they will be chosen by chance. In case we need to get in touch with you again, as far as you know will you be living at this address this time next year?

                    Yes (RECORD NAME, ADDRESS, TELEPHONE NUMBER BELOW)... 1

                    No (RECORD NAME, TELEPHONE NUMBER. GET BEST POSSIBLE ADDRESS AND OBTAIN MAILING ADDRESS IF "R" IS IN RURAL AREA. RECORD BELOW.) 2

Respondent's Name:_____

Address:_____
            Number   Street

        _____
              City   State   Zip

Telephone Number: (_____) _____
                   Area Code   Number

H-38.   In case you should move unexpectedly, would you please give me the names of two close relatives or friends who would be likely to know where you can be reached? (ENTER NAMES BELOW, THEN ASK H-39 to H-43.)

		Name	Name
H-39.	How is (PERSON) related to you?	_____ Relationship	_____ Relationship
H-40.	What is (his/her) address?	No. Street _____ City _____ State Zip	No. Street _____ City _____ State Zip
H-41.	What is (his/her) telephone number?	(_____) _____ Area Code Number	(_____) _____ Area Code Number
H-42.	Is (PERSON) now married?	Yes .... 1 No 2	Yes .... 1 No 2
H-43.	(IF YES): What is (her husband's/his wife's) full name?	_____ Name	_____ Name

Time Ended: _____ am/pm

As I mentioned there are two other very important parts to this study being conducted. One part is that we will be going to the schools to find out what students are being taught. In order to do this the school requires a signed Parental Consent Form.

GET PARENTAL CONSENT FORM SIGNED FOR EACH SELECTED CHILD

The second part to this study is an interview with [TARGET CHILD(REN)] to assess English language abilities. Another person skilled in education will be coming to do this. Could you tell me the best time for this person to return?

Best time for tester to call: _____

APPENDIX C

PARENTAL CONSENT FORM

Parental Consent Form

Dear Principal:

You, or the school official you appoint, have my permission to fill out the attached questionnaire about my child. I also give you permission to provide the answers to (name of firm).

I understand that:

- the answers will be used in the Children's English and Services Study; and
- this study is being conducted by L. Miranda and Associates, Inc. with Westat, Inc./RDI for education agencies in the Department of Health, Education, and Welfare.

I have been made fully aware of the care being taken by the firm named above to protect the information you provide about my child. I understand that:

- only the people who work on this study will see the answers; and
- my child's name will not appear with the answers when the results are reported.

I also understand that the information is being asked to help improve schooling for children who come from homes where a language other than English is spoken.

I have kept a copy of this form.

(Name of Child)	*(Print Your Full Name)*

(Age)	*(Grade)*	*(Your Signature)*

(School Name)	*(Relationship to Child)*

(District Name)	*(Date)*

(School Address)

White Copy - School
Yellow Copy - Intv.
Pink Copy - Signer

(City)   *(State)*

Forma de Consentimiento

Al principal de la Escuela,

Usted o el funcionario escolar que seleccione tendrá mi permiso para llenar el cuestionario sobre mi hijo/a. También tiene mi consentimiento para responderle a las respuestas que (*compañía*) le haga.

Tengo por entendido que:

● las respuestas serán utilizadas en el Estudio Infantil sobre el Inglés y Servicios; y que,

● este estudio se está llevando a cabo por L. Miranda & Associates, Inc. con Westat, Inc./ RDI para las agencias de educación del Departamento de Salud, Educación y Bienestar.

Estoy bajo el completo entendimiento que las firmas antes mencionadas tomarán las precauciones necesarias para no divulgar la información que reciban sobre my hijo/a. Entiendo que:

● solamente las personas que trabajan en este estudio verán las respuestas; y que

● el nombre de mi hijo/a no aparecerá con las respuestas cuando se den a conocer los resultados.

También tengo entendido que la información que se obtenga en este estudio ayudará a mejorar la educación de los niños que vienen de hogares donde se habla otro idioma que no sea el inglés.

He retenido una copia de esta forma.

_____	_____
(Name of Child)	*(Print Your Full Name)*
_____ _____	_____
(Age) *(Grade)*	*(Your Signature)*
_____	_____
(School Name)	*(Relationship to Child)*
_____	_____
(District Name)	*(Date)*
_____	
(School Address)	

White Copy - School
Yellow Copy - Intv.
Pink Copy - Signer

_____
(City)   *(State)*

APPENDIX D

COMMENTS FROM REVIEWERS

March 31, 1982

Dr. Dan Ulibarri, Research Associate
National Institute of Education
Mail Stop 6
1200 19th Street, N.W.
Washington, DC 20208

Dear Dr. Ulibarri:

I am enclosing my comments on the report entitled *Educational Needs Assessment for Language Minority Children with Limited English Proficiency in the United States,* by J. Michael O'Malley. Basically, my comments relate to some basic policy implications that I see as a result of this report.

First of all, the fact that only one-third of limited English proficient children are being served in bilingual education programs is a very important observation. Furthermore, of the 34% who are being served in some capacity, an estimated 83% of those children are limited English proficient. This is important because the charge is often made that children who are in these programs don't really need to be in them.

You need to remember that in the State of California it is required by law that at least one-third of the students in bilingual education classrooms NOT be limited English proficient. This is written specifically to insure balanced classrooms, whereby an approximate two-thirds to one-third ratio of students who are limited English proficient to students who are fluent English proficient would be maintained.

The second observation I have has to do with the conclusion that the bilingual education programs that were being provided through Federal or State support did *not* appear to focus on maintaining the child's native language. Probably the most constant criticism that we receive in bilingual education is that we are perpetuating the child's native language at the sake of teaching him or her English quickly. This report clearly points out that instructional time is not at the expense of learning English.

A third observation is that children in bilingual education programs are receiving approximately the same amount of English language instruction as those who are NOT in bilingual education programs. To me, this is the most significant issue in this report. If children are receiving the same amount of instruction in the English language, then the key difference is in the amount of subject area that they are learning in their native language. Time is on our side. Ultimately I believe that it will be proven beyond a shadow of a doubt that children in bilingual education classes are getting a superior education.

I think it is important that children served in bilingual education programs are primarily in the early elementary grades. The fallacy that once a child is enrolled in bilingual education programs, he or she stays there forever just doesn't hold true. Clearly there is a decrease in the numbers of students in bilingual education programs as you proceed through the grade levels.

Last, I think it was important to indicate that the students in bilingual education programs were primarily administered tests of the English language. Barely a quarter of them were given tests in their native language. I believe this fact alone spells out the emphasis in our programs on the acquisition of English language and not on the maintenance of non-English languages.

Dr. Dan Ulibarri
National Institute of Education
March 31, 1982

I hope these comments are helpful to you. I am sorry that they are so late in arriving, but we had a few problems to cope with in California.

Best of luck to you in getting this report. Please let me know if there is anything else that we can do to assist you.

Sincerely yours,

Olivia Martínez
Administrator
San Jose Unified School District

February 16, 1982

Dr. Dan Ulibarri
Research Associate, Teaching &
   Learning
National Institute of Education
Mail Stop 6
1200 19th Street, N.W.
Washington, DC 20208

Dear Dan:

I reviewed the "Educational Needs Assessment for Language Minority Children with Limited English Proficiency" report with considerable interest.

For purposes of responding to your requested critique I have addressed two categories of concern: (1) policy issues, and (2) technical/editorial issues.

Regarding policy issues, the report does provide interesting data to guide subsequent studies. It does not, however, adequately answer the Congressional mandate—the data are too old (1978), too limited in terms of sample size (less than five hundredths of one percent for California), and because of poor operational definitions the data are not meaningfully, nor appropriately, analyzed.

Equally important, I question what appears to be an implicit assumption of the study—that somehow "bilingual education" is not detracting from English acquisition. The important issue is that LEP students attain academic skills and mastery of English over a reasonable period of time. I firmly believe that ultimate attainment of English literacy skills may require (for some students) instruction principally or even exclusively in the primary language for a period of time. Since language skills are interdependent and there is a common underlying proficiency among languages, time spent building primary language skills lays the foundation for eventual attainment of English literacy skills. It is, therefore, misleading and overly simplistic merely to measure the amount of time spent in English and the primary language. At some stages in a bilingual education program the balance of time in each language might favor the primary language, and this—contrary to popular opinion—will actually foster better eventual attainment of English skills than a program that provides the child with too much time in non-comprehensible English.

California counted 233,444 LES/NES pupils in 1977–78. The study obtained pupil data on only 114 pupils in California, for a sample size of only .05%. These 114 pupils were an even smaller sample of the 594,000 LEP pupils estimated by the CESS report.

In brief, without elaboration of the theoretical premises of bilingual education regarding primary language use, the report runs afoul of the risk of overstating the meaning of the data.

Regarding technical/editorial points, the report requires further work to ensure accuracy and meaningful labeling of tables. Specific comments are as follows:

1.   Preface—no comments.

Dr. Dan Ulibarri
Research Associate,
  Teaching & Learning
February 16, 1982
Page Two

2.   Executive Summary

 ● The narrative should include sample size data. It is difficult to ascertain significance of data presented as percentges without actual Ns.

 ● Listing findings in the manner presented makes digestion of the implications difficult because so much is presented. Consider simplifying the presentation by focusing on key findings.

 ● On page viii, item 5, a statement is made that 24% of LEP pupils receive assistance under Title I; 7%, Title VII; 14%, state support; and 5%, other. This adds up to 50%—what, if any, is the source of other funding?

 ● Also on page ix, reference to "bilingual types of instruction" (line 6 from top) is unclear. Although defined elsewhere, it gives a somewhat erroneous impression. Consider a glossary or define.

 ● On page xi, items 3–4, concerning rating appear to be contradictory. Item 3 states that 22% of LEPs were able to use English well and 19% were rated able to use English adequately, but item 4 states 52% of LEPs were rated as one-half year or more below grade level. The point here is when the percentages presented in the items are compared, they don't necessarily add up.

3.   Source of Data

 ● Note should be made of response rates.

4.   Accuracy of Data

 ● The text notes that "all figures provided in this report are estimates of what would be estimated with a complete census." I'm not sure such a statement is justified in light of some of the small sample sizes as well as initial difficulties in securing the data.

5.   Introduction—No major comments.

 ● However, note should be made here, or elsewhere, that data are based on a 1978 CESS report; that is, here it is 1982 and we're dealing with outdated data.

6.   Conceptual Framework

 ● I'm concerned that Texas and California samples are underrepresented, which produces grave problems in "weighing" non-response (Table II–1, page 7). Given the fact that the pupil N is only 990, much ado is made of the high response rate of 67% (excluding Texas)—the fact is the total response was very low; in other words, the response rate is relative to the pupil sample size.

7A. Results

- I concur with the limitations set forth [pages 9–10, 2–4].

- It is important, I believe, to define "instructional type" [p. 10] operationally. Since English language instruction (ELI) does not use L_1 as an instructional medium (as is the case with ESL), why is it included? The differentiation based on cultural activities only is precarious. (Does "professional staffing" [p. 10] mean a certified bilingual teacher?)

- The findings that fewer than 1% of pupils sampled received bilingual instruction is as striking as it is frightening. This conclusion should be highlighted—it is certainly contrary to the purposes of program funding.

- On page 12, 2nd paragraph, note is made of "297 thousand, or 17% . . . (and) an estimated 189,000 or 11%. . . ." I do not see the justification in use of these figures—are they extractions/projections of the percentages? Stick with the actual Ns. The projections are precarious at best.

7B. Characteristics of Instructional Types

- Grade Distribution—no comment.

- Sources of Support—The totals in the narrative do not equal 100%. LEPs in bilingual programs receiving funding from ESEA Title I, Migrant Title I, and ESEA Title VII equal 59%. Similarly, 28% of LEPs in English instruction programs receive funding from these programs. Can one assume that the balance receives either no support, or some State support? The non-Federal support figures don't match. Also note is made that USOE's figures are based on grant proposals—are these the total number of proposals that are submitted, or are they funded proposals?

7C. Levels of Instruction

- Information on hours of instruction is particularly important (i.e., only 17% of LEPs receive 5 hours + of non-English instruction). These data should be highlighted, but in the context of the earlier conclusion that fewer than 1% receive minimally accepted levels of services.

- Staffing—without detailed rationale/criteria of "professional staffing" this information is of uncertain value. The criteria should have been State bilingual certification.

- Language Assessment—no comment.

7D. Indices of Educational Need

- Subject Area Assessment—no comment.

- School Classification—School self-ratings are precarious; the qualifications of the six categories are subjective. Although interesting, it's difficult to make any substantive conclusions.

- Reading Achievement—School ratings precarious.

- Grade Retention—These data provide an insight into grade retention and are certainly of value. I regard this as quite informative since it has not been generated before. The cause of grade retention, however, merits exploration.

8. Conclusion

- As with any report of this nature deriving conclusions is difficult. A considerable amount of data is presented—some substantive, others precarious—which makes definitive conclusions impossible. As previously noted, the data are relatively old—1978—and are based on a limited sample. Therefore, it would appear best to be tentative in the conclusions. The data provide helpful insights as to numbers of LEPs, services, etc., that of necessity should be further explored by other studies.

What can be said with some degree of confidence is that bilingual programs in size, scope, and quality may not be reaching those in most need. The configurations of the data are certainly contrary to those alleged in the popular press. It is regrettable that the amount of data is not sufficiently large, nor better operationalized. Because of the lack of substantive information, the generalizability of the conclusions is pre-empted.

Sincerely,

Robert A. Cervantes
Assistant Administrator
Office of Bilingual Bicultural
   Education
State of California Department of Education

MEMORANDUM   March 15, 1982

TO: Dan Ulibarri
FROM: Celia Zavala Castañeda
RE: Observations—"Educational Needs Assessment for Language Minority
           Children with Limited English Proficiency" by J. Michael O'Malley

These written comments are in response to your request during our discussion of the above report in the telephone conversation with you and Olivia Martínez.

First, I want to acknowledge that the design of the survey is thoughtful and takes into account the salient issues that concern most educators who provide services to limited English proficient students.

My concern regarding the size of the national sample which excludes Texas and underrepresents California impels me to call attention to the need to use caution in the interpretation of the data as truly representative of the national scene if it is to be used to shape national policy discussions.

However, the author's summary and conclusions point out these same limitations. (One would tend to see them as external to the study.)

If one is to make assumptions, these might follow:

1. The national census of LEP students is underrepresented.

2. If the districts that responded offer some special services for LEP students, what assumptions can one infer from (a) those who chose not to, and (b) those who reported not having obtained permission to release data in time?

Concerns:

1. That the schools are so diversified in the identification process of LEP students and assessing their needs.

2. That so many schools have no data for the LEP students and others have inadequate systems for collecting data.

3. That resources to these children are limited especially in retaining personnel with specialized training.

4. That the mother language and culture of the LEPs are taken so little into account in light of all the recent findings that indicate the need to include them in order to augment the learning of English with the result of equal assimilation into the educational mainstream.

5. That only 23% of those students in the sample received bilingual bicultural services as defined by the National Task Force (Miranda) and 58% of the sample received English-only instruction with no cultural references or instruction of the mother tongue does not speak well for the schools in meeting the two national goals:

   a. providing equal educational opportunity

   b. promoting unity and harmony among diverse groups.

Also, it appears that schools received monies from outside sources as the primary support for providing educational services; furthermore, it's alarming that the support was primarily of a compensatory nature, e.g., Title I: 24% of the LEP sample.

Only 7% received Title VII funds, which one assumes require a non-compensatory thrust, but only 5% received local support or support from other souces. The support from the State government, however, seems to have been fairly good.

It appears that the national attitude toward language minority students has changed very little since the inception of the Bilingual Education Act.

However, I would like to draw your attention to the finding that *may dispel the notion that bilingual education programs do not teach English to children*. The data showed that for students receiving bilingual bicultural instruction, 35% received 5–9 hours of English instruction a week and 48% received 10 hours or more a week. There was no difference between the students who received instruction in English only; i.e., 28% received 5 to 9 hours of English instruction a week and 48% *received 10 hours or more*.

Another concern is in relation to the grade distribution of LEP students in the survey. The largest numbers appear to be in the early years (K–6) and grow smaller toward the higher grades. This could reflect the disproportionate number of dropouts that continue to characterize the LEP population.

An interesting observation is that when the study used the National Task Force criteria for testing L_1 the statistics vary, i.e., they were lower. An example: of the 43% of the LEP students receiving bilingual instruction only 23% received assessment to identify mother tongue proficiency. The statistics drop to 5% when the instruments for measuring L_1 are rated using the criteria established by the Task Force.

Another concern is that schools tended to overrate the LEP students' proficiency in English.

Equally alarming is that overall performance of LEP students on English reading relative to NLEP students of the same language group is below grade level:

   16%—one-half to 1 year below grade level
   13%—close to 1 full year below grade level
   23%—more than 1 full year below grade level

The survey reports that LEP students are characterized by high grade retention and overagedness (2 years or more above grade). This is of great concern to us because of the psychological and socio-cultural implications that impact on these students' motivation to learn.

It appears that we need to assess the correlation between grade retention, overagedness, and the degree of effective assessment and instruction in L_1 for LEP students as well as the cultural factors in curriculum and instruction.

I look at the results of this study as a first step in the examination of assumptions that the results appear to suggest.

What is the total future for LEP students?

What steps should be taken to insure appropriate identification and assessment of needs and mother tongue proficiency?

What are the appropriate instructional programs?

What is the relationship of instruction in the native tongue to learning English?

What are the factors for lower LEP student count at the higher grades?

What are the culturally relevant factors to curriculum?

APPENDIX E

CHILDREN'S ENGLISH AND SERVICES STUDY: EXECUTIVE SUMMARY

EXECUTIVE SUMMARY

LANGUAGE MINORITY CHILDREN WITH LIMITED
ENGLISH PROFICIENCY IN THE UNITED STATES

SPRING 1978

An estimated 2.4 million children with limited English language proficiency aged 5-14 years were living in the United States in the Spring of 1978. This number represents 63% of all children aged 5-14 years living in households where a language other than English was spoken. In addition, there were estimated to be as many as 1.2 million limited English proficient children younger or older than the 5-14 year olds but also of school age. The number of limited English proficient children aged 5-14 was estimated from the first study of its scope ever conducted in the United States to determine the number of language minority children with limited English proficiency.

Limited English language proficiency was found to be more prevalent among children living in households where Spanish was spoken and among children in three major states as contrasted with the remainder of the country. However, limited English proficiency did not differ markedly by age. The findings are discussed in detail below.

RESULTS BY LANGUAGE

More children aged 5-14 years living in households where Spanish was spoken were limited in English proficiency compared to children of the same age living in households where other non-English languages were spoken.

- There were 1.7 million Spanish language background children aged 5-14 years with limited English proficiency. This was 73% of the total number of children in this age range living in households where Spanish was spoken.

- There were .7 million children aged 5-14 years from all other language minority backgrounds combined with limited English proficiency. This was 47% of the total number of children in this age range living in households where other non-English languages were spoken.

RESULTS BY AGE

The percentage of limited English proficient children among all children living in households where a language other than English was spoken did not differ markedly by age. The following percentages are for various age groups, for all languages combined:

5-6 year olds:	67% limited in English
7-8 year olds:	68% limited in English
9-11 year olds:	59% limited in English
12-14 year olds:	61% limited in English

RESULTS BY STATE

An estimated 1.5 million or 62% of all limited English proficient children lived in three states: California, Texas, and New York. The figures by state are as follows for all languages combined:

California	594,000 limited in English
New York	468,000 limited in English
Texas	438,000 limited in English
Remainder of U.S.	908,000 limited in English
Total	2,408,000 limited in English

New York had the highest percentage of children who were limited in English proficiency among children aged 5-14 years living in households where a language other than English was spoken. The figures are:

New York	77% limited in English
California	70% limited in English
Texas	70% limited in English
Remainder of U.S.	53% limited in English
Total	63% limited in English

SOURCE OF DATA

The Children's English and Services Study was conducted under contract from the National Institute of Education with shared support from the National Center for Education Statistics and the U.S. Office of Education. The study was designed to respond to a Congressional mandate in the Bilingual Education Act (Elementary and Secondary Education Act, Title VII) to count the number of children with limited English speaking ability in the United States. The work was carried out by a consortium headed by L. Miranda & Associates, Inc., of Washington, D.C. as prime contractor.[1]

Adults were interviewed in the Spring of 1978 in a nationally representative sample of approximately 35,000 households. About 2,200 households were identified where a language other than English was spoken and where children between the ages of 5 and 14 were living. Within these households, selected children were individually administered a test in English that determined whether or not the child was limited in English language proficiency. The sample was designed to provide representative numbers of children in California, Texas, New York, and the remainder of the country.

The test in English was designed to meet the definition of limited English proficiency in the Bilingual Education Act. Representatives of 30 State Education Agencies developed specifications for the test and served on a review team for the study. The reviewers found that no existing test would meet the Congressional intent. They urged development of a test measuring age-specific speaking, listening, reading, and writing skills in English. The test criterion for limited English proficiency is a cut-off point on the total score that accu-

---

1. Retrieval of CESS data tapes and accompanying documentation is being arranged through the following sources: Reference Service Machine Readable Archives Division—NNR, National Archives and Records Service, Washington, D.C. 20408 (telephone 202/724-1080); and Inter-University Consortium for Political and Social Research, P.O. Box 1248, Ann Arbor, Mich. 48106.

rately classifies children as limited or not limited in English for their age level. The criterion was derived from field work with an independent sample.

The Children's English and Services Study is one of a number of studies undertaken by the Education Division of the Department of Health, Education, and Welfare to assess educational needs and to improve instructional effectiveness for limited English proficient children.

ACCURACY OF THE DATA

Because the results are based on a sample rather than a census of the population, all figures provided in this report are estimates with an error range within which the true score may lie with a 95% level of confidence. Examples of the error range follow.

The national estimate of limited English proficient children aged 5-14 years is 2.4 million. The number 2.4 million is 63% of all children in the age range 5-14 living in households where a language other than English is spoken, with a range from 55% to 71% at a 95% level of confidence.

METHODOLOGICAL REVIEW

A methodological review of this report was prepared by the National Center for Education Statistics (NCES), Office for Research Analysis (ORA).[2] In the review, three analytical issues were discussed:

- Were the items which were selected for inclusion in the Language Measurement and Assessment Inventory (LM&AI) selected properly?

- Were the cutoff scores for the LM&AI, which were determined and used to classify children as either English proficient or of limited English proficiency (LEP), set properly?

- What were the effects of nonresponse bias on the counts and estimates of LEP children?

Accordingly, NCES/ORA offered the following recommendations:

1. There should be a caveat concerning the limitations of the CESS results "which are a function of the current state-of-the-art in the assessment of language proficiency."

2. Using an alternative analytic procedure NCES/ORA reported a 9.22% higher estimate of LEP children. Their recommendation was to include this information in the report.

3. In regard to nonresponse bias, NCES/ORA concluded "that further investigations. . .are not warranted."

---

2. *Children's English and Services Study: Estimates of Limited English Proficient Children in the United States— Methodological Reviews,* published by the National Clearinghouse for Bilingual Education (Rosslyn, Virginia), 1982.

Issues concerning the state-of-the-art in language proficiency assessment in general are discussed in the NCES document. A response to NCES/ORA estimation procedures, however, has been prepared by the National Institute of Education (NIE). The NCES/ORA review and NIE response may be accessed through the National Clearinghouse for Bilingual Education.

☆ U. S. GOVERNMENT PRINTING OFFICE : 1982 379-293